'Parallel Play'

RE-IMAGINING CULTURAL ICONS

Think of it as a masquerade ball where our invited guests are none other than some of the most influential figures in history.

These are individuals who left indelible imprints on our collective consciousness, men and women who shaped our world with their talents, their courage, their genius, and their charisma.

But tonight, they step into our grand ball wearing not their usual attire, but the garb of athletes, each donning a sport or activity that best echoes their personalities, their traits, their essence.

So, let's flip the coin and explore the other side, the side where our late icons are not just heroes in their respective fields, but also in arenas they could have conquered. Welcome to 'Parallel Play.' Let the games begin."

ICONS

Inside:

Marilyn
Monroe

Frank
Sinatra

Richard
Pryor

Bruce Lee on a drum set, his hands a blur, producing rhythms as powerful and precise as his martial arts moves.

Bob
Marley

Michael
Jackson

Muhammad Ali, the boxing legend, not in a ring but on a stage, crooning songs as effortlessly as he used to throw punches, his voice as captivating as his persona.

Elizabeth
Taylor

Martin
Luther
King

Jimi Hendrix, surfing in the Pacific North West, with a wind blown afro in harmony with. ocean waves.

Steven
Jobs

Nelson
Mandela

Princess
Di

Abe
Lincoln

PELE

GHANDI

PRINCE

KOBE

Malcolm X

EINSTEIN

ARETHA

JFK

ELVIS

BRANDO

TUPAC

As we journey through these pages, you will meet such dopplegangers, figures familiar yet intriguingly different.

Maya Angelou

Kurt Cobain

Howard Hughes

Bette Davis

Robin Williams

Winston Chruchill

Little Richard

Billy Graham

James Dean

SECRETARIAT

THE ART:

The lines between reality and fantasy blur as we delve into this unique experiment of aesthetics, combining the grainy texture of old films with the ethereal quality of digital art.

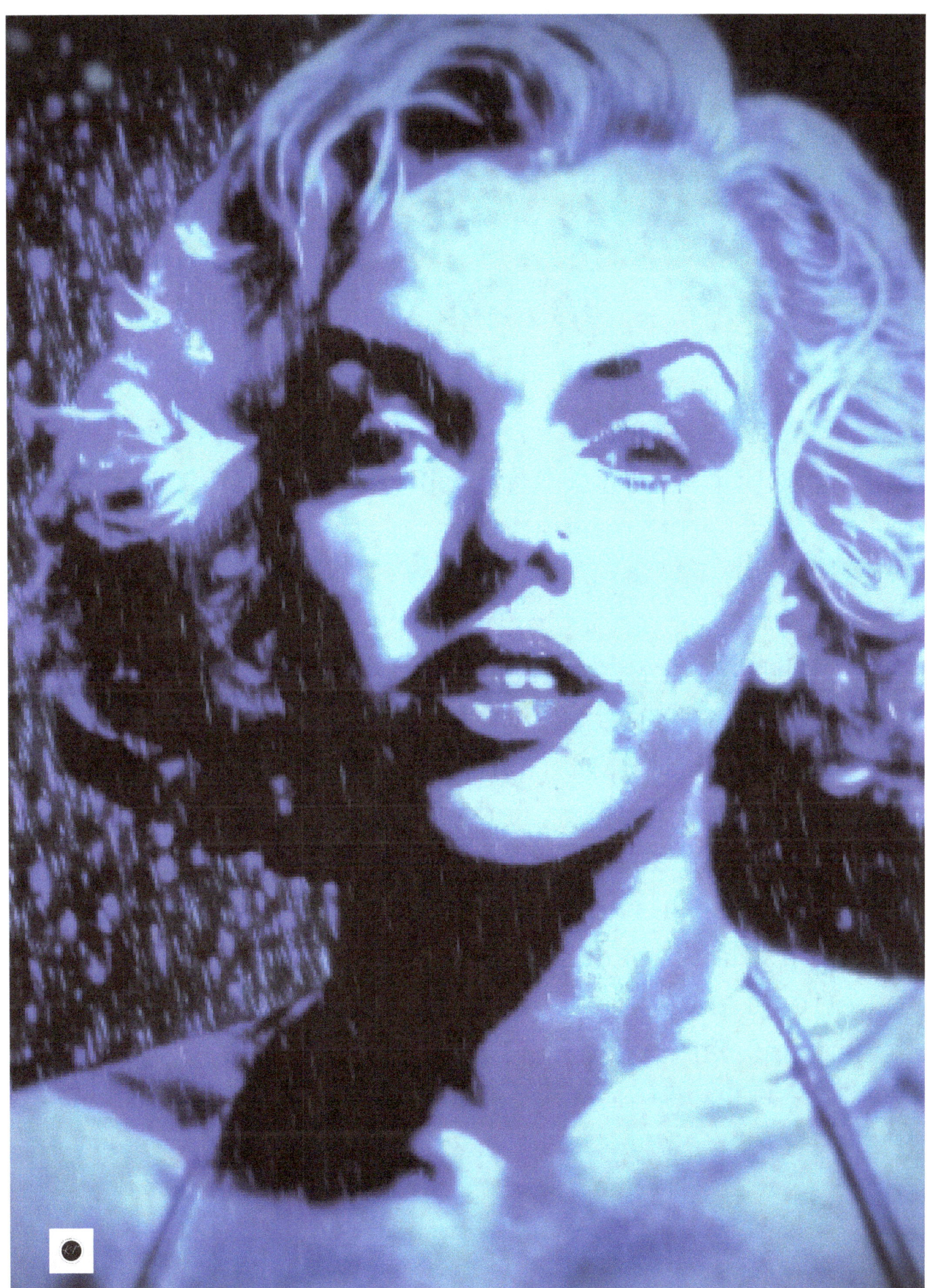

Marilyn Monroe

Marilyn Monroe as a softball player would emphasize her strength, determination, and ability to captivate audiences with her charm and charisma. Softball requires power, coordination, and teamwork, which aligns with Monroe's talent as an actress, model, and cultural icon.

As a softball player, Marilyn Monroe would showcase her resilience, focus, and adaptability, much like how she captivated audiences around the world with her memorable roles and distinctive persona. This also highlights her capacity for concentration, her ability to perform and, perseverance, as softball games can be intense and demand both physical and mental fortitude.

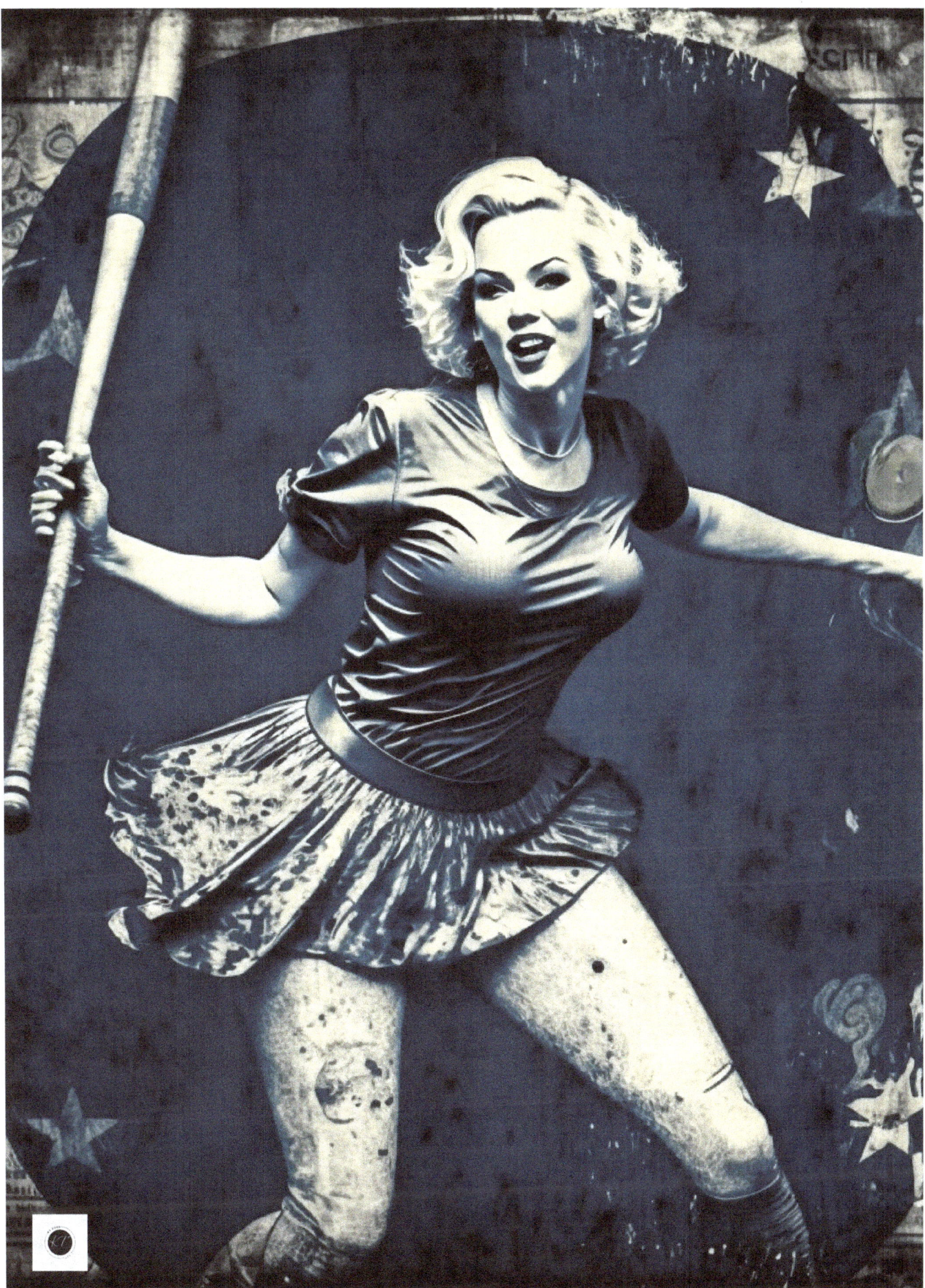

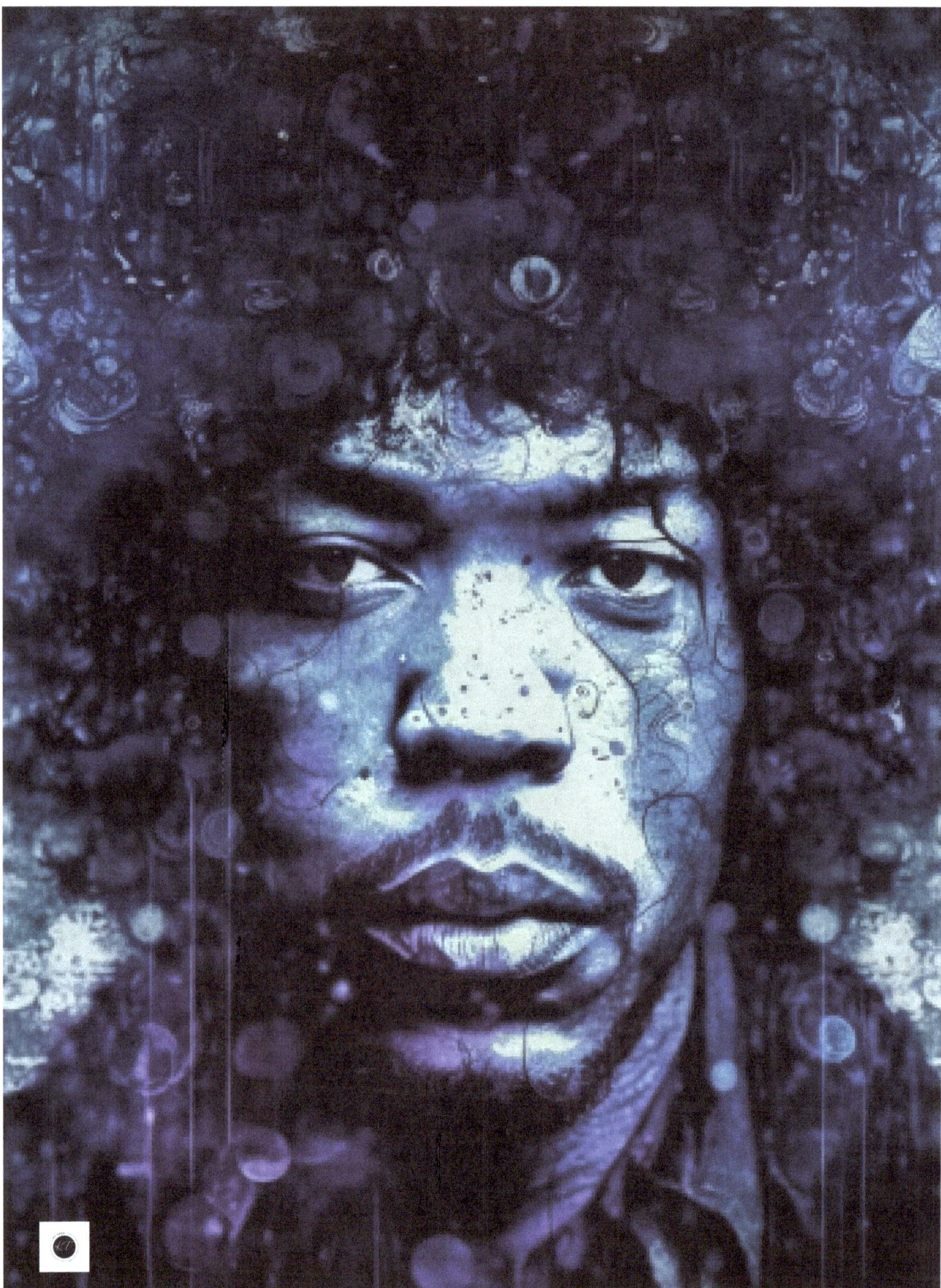

Jimi Hendrix

Jimi Hendrix as a surfer would emphasize his free-spirited nature, creativity, and ability to navigate challenging situations with grace and style. Surfing requires balance, adaptability, and a connection with the natural elements, which aligns with Hendrix's talent as a groundbreaking guitarist.

As a surfer, Jimi Hendrix would showcase his fearlessness, focus, and adaptability, much like how he captivated audiences around the world with his innovative guitar playing and revolutionary approach to music. This role would also highlight his capacity for pushing boundaries, his affinity for improvisation, as surfing demands the skill to ride unpredictable waves and adjust to changing conditions.

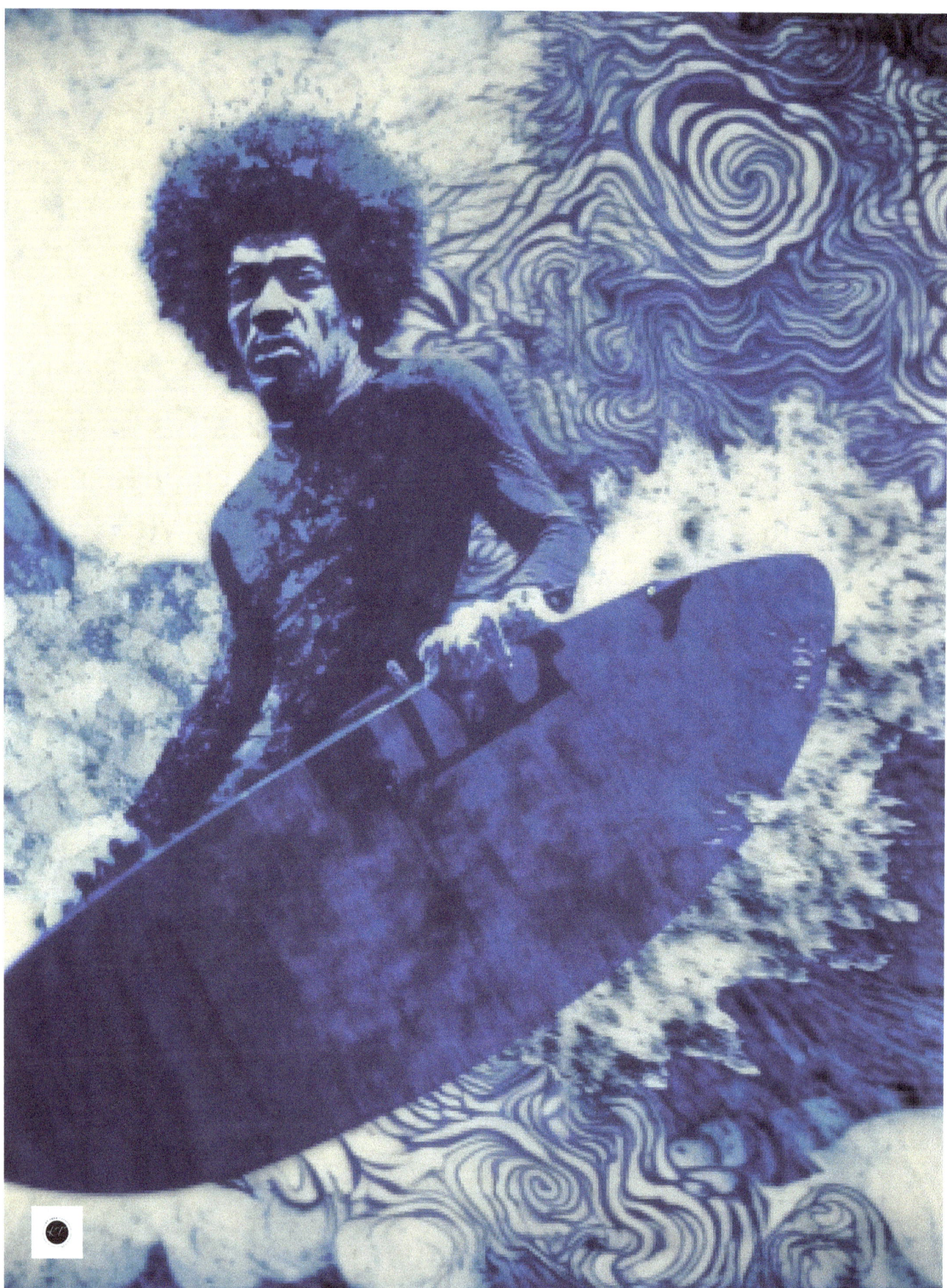

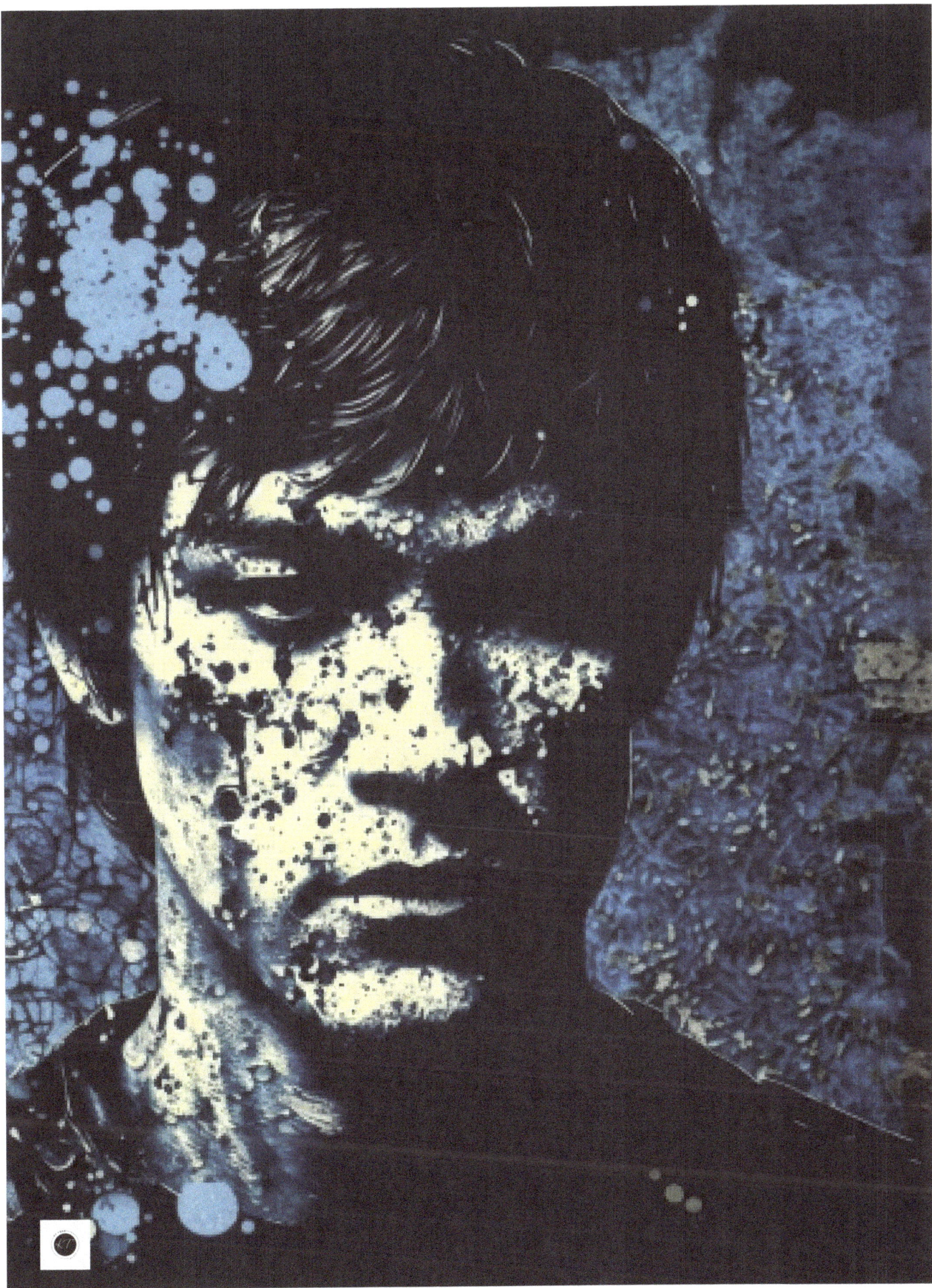

Bruce Lee

Bruce Lee as a drummer would emphasize his exceptional sense of timing, precision, and ability to entertain audiences through his incredible performances. Drumming is an art form that requires a combination of rhythm, coordination, and power, which aligns with Lee's talent as a martial artist, actor, and philosopher.

As a drummer, Bruce Lee would showcase his impeccable timing, focus, and adaptability, much like how he captivated audiences around the world with his groundbreaking martial arts techniques and movies. This role also highlights his capacity for concentration, his ability to excel in high-pressure situations, and his dedication to mastery, as drumming demands consistent practice and commitment to perfect one's skills.

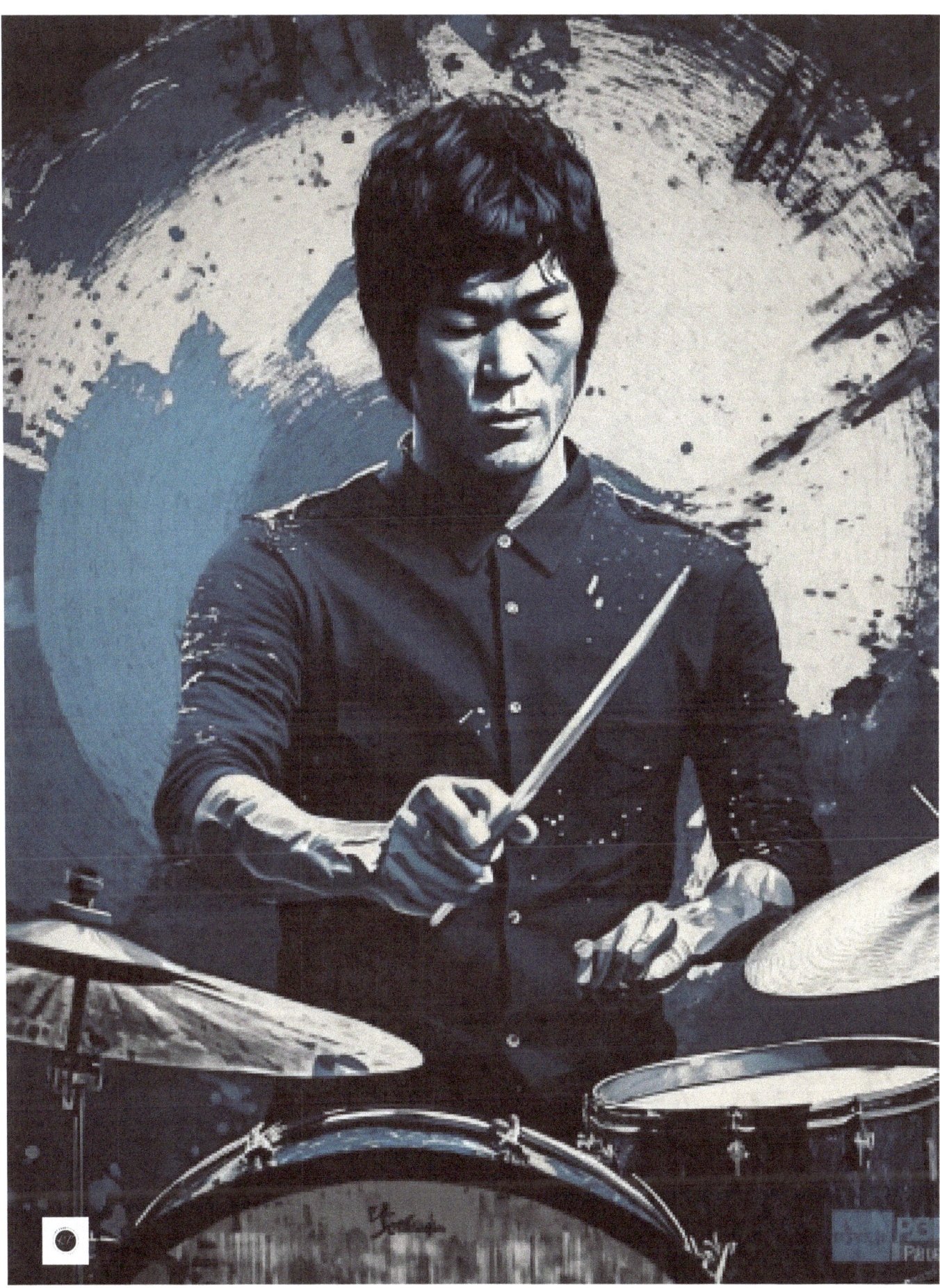

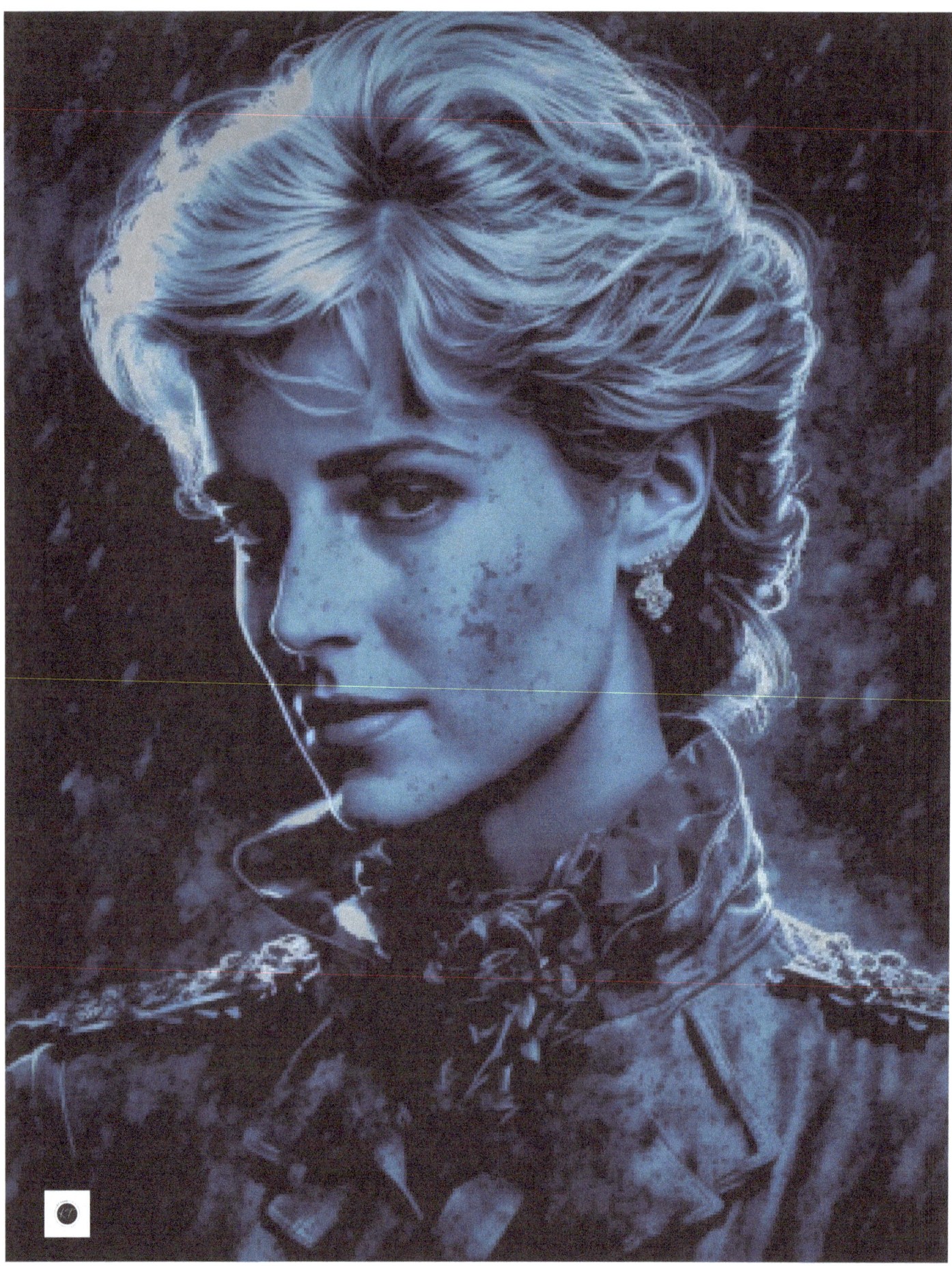

Princess Di

As an equestrian, Princess Diana would showcase her elegance, focus, and adaptability, much like how she captivated the hearts of people around the world with her kindness, style, and dedication to various charitable causes.

This role would also highlight her capacity for building strong connections, her ability to perform under pressure, and her resilience, as equestrian sports can be challenging and require a deep understanding between the rider and the horse.

The choice of equestrianism as her "sport" would reflect the refined, powerful, and relationship-oriented aspects of her work, as well as her ability to inspire people with her warmth and her enduring presence.

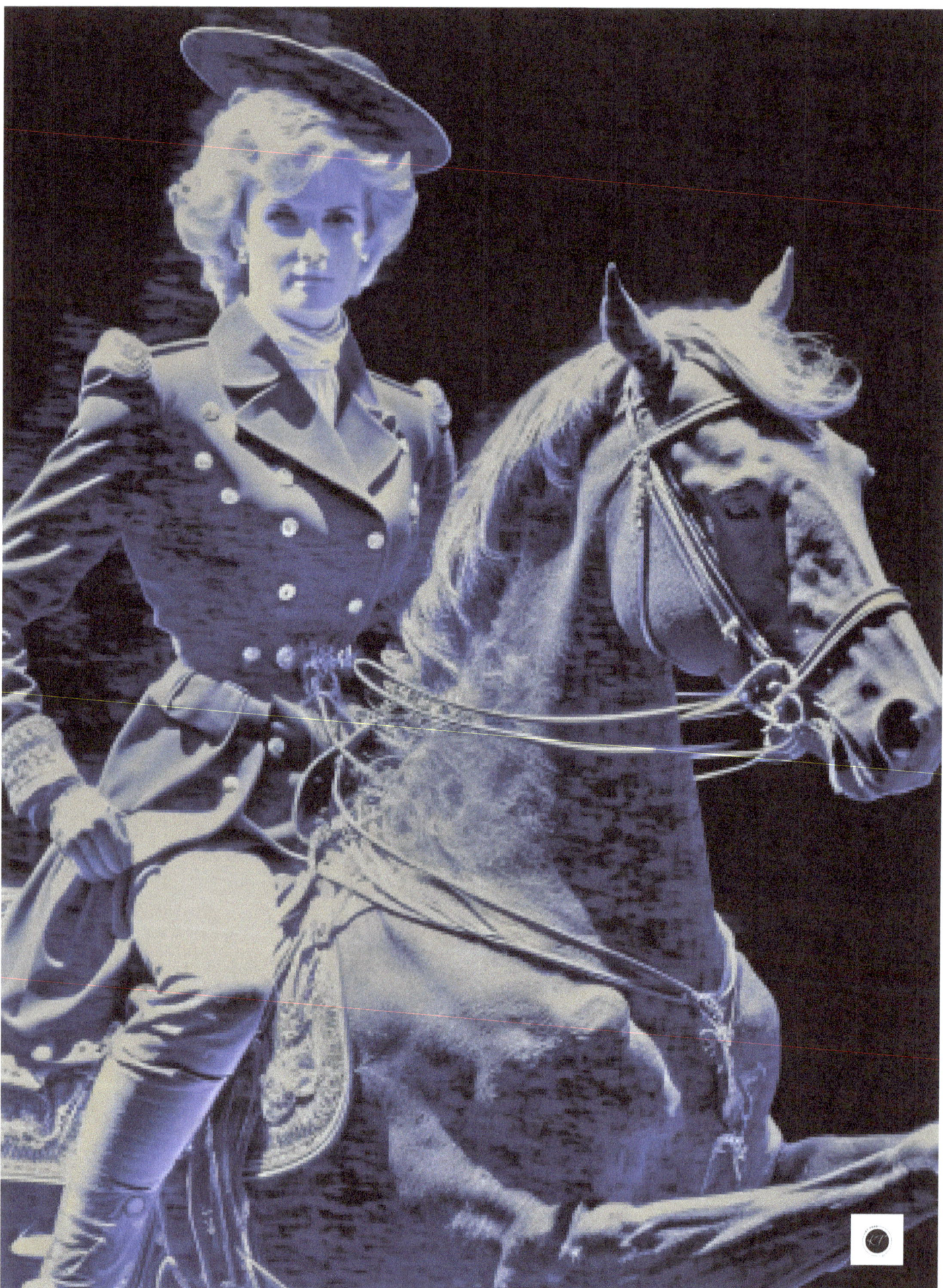

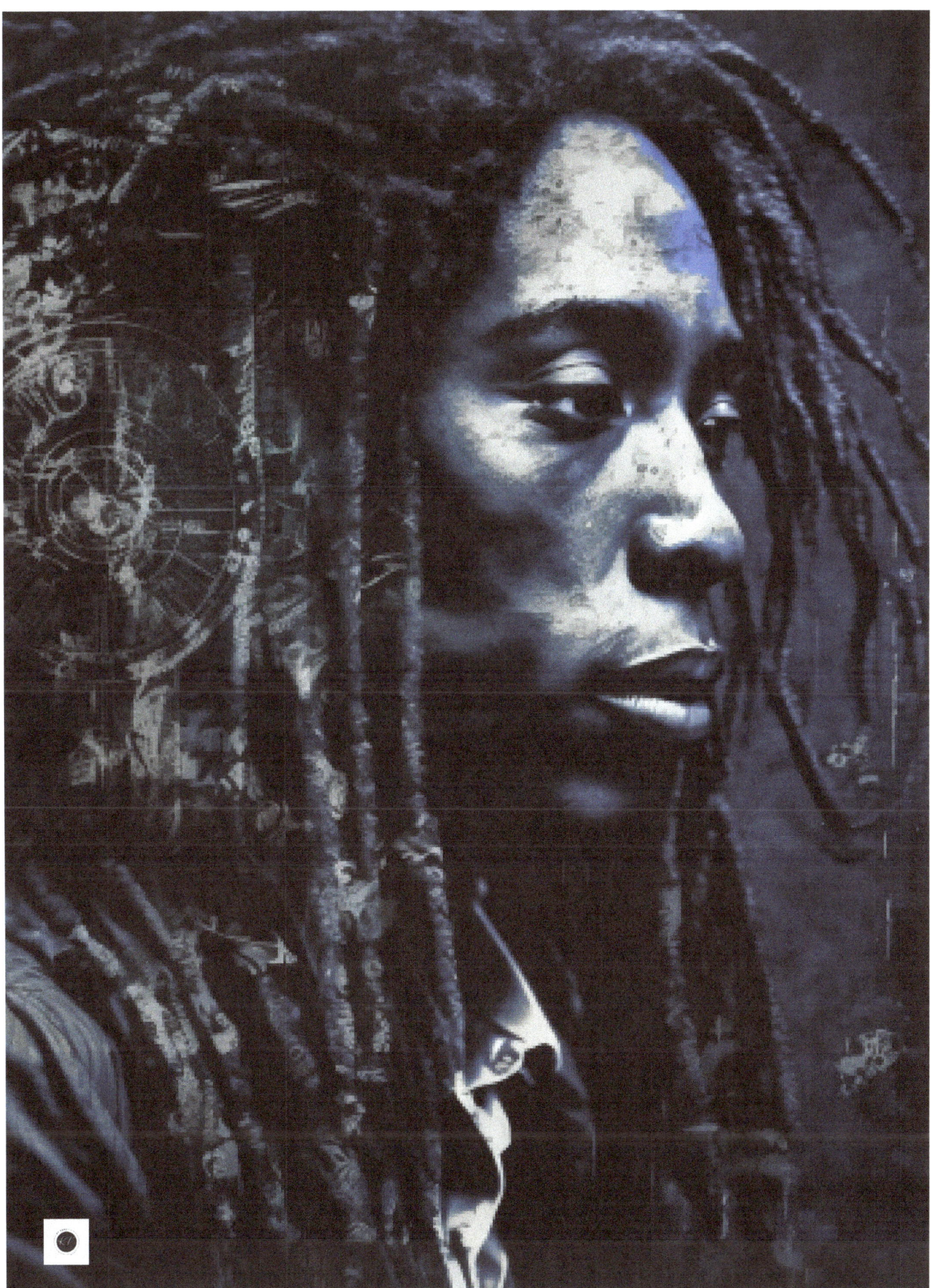

Bob Marley

Bob Marley as a soccer player would emphasize his passion, energy, and teamwork. Soccer requires a combination of physical fitness, coordination, and collaboration, which aligns with Marley's talent as a musician and his impact as a cultural icon.

As a soccer player, Bob Marley would showcase his determination, focus, and adaptability, much like how he captivated audiences around the world with his music and his message of unity, love, and social change.

This role highlights his capacity for connecting with people and love for the game (as Marley was known to be an avid soccer fan and player in real life), and his ability to inspire others, as soccer is a sport that relies on teamwork and shared goals. Yeah, shared gooooaaallls!

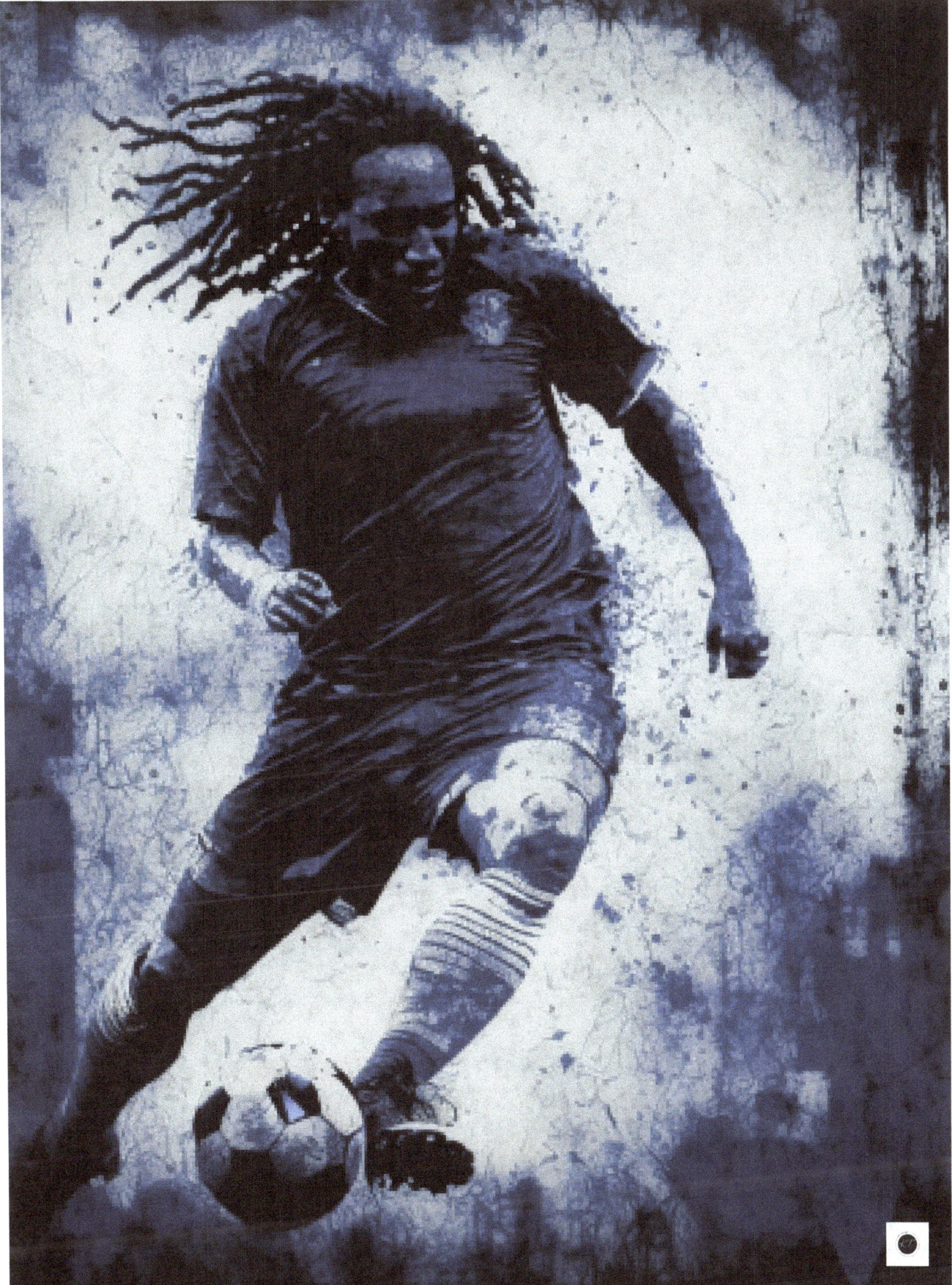

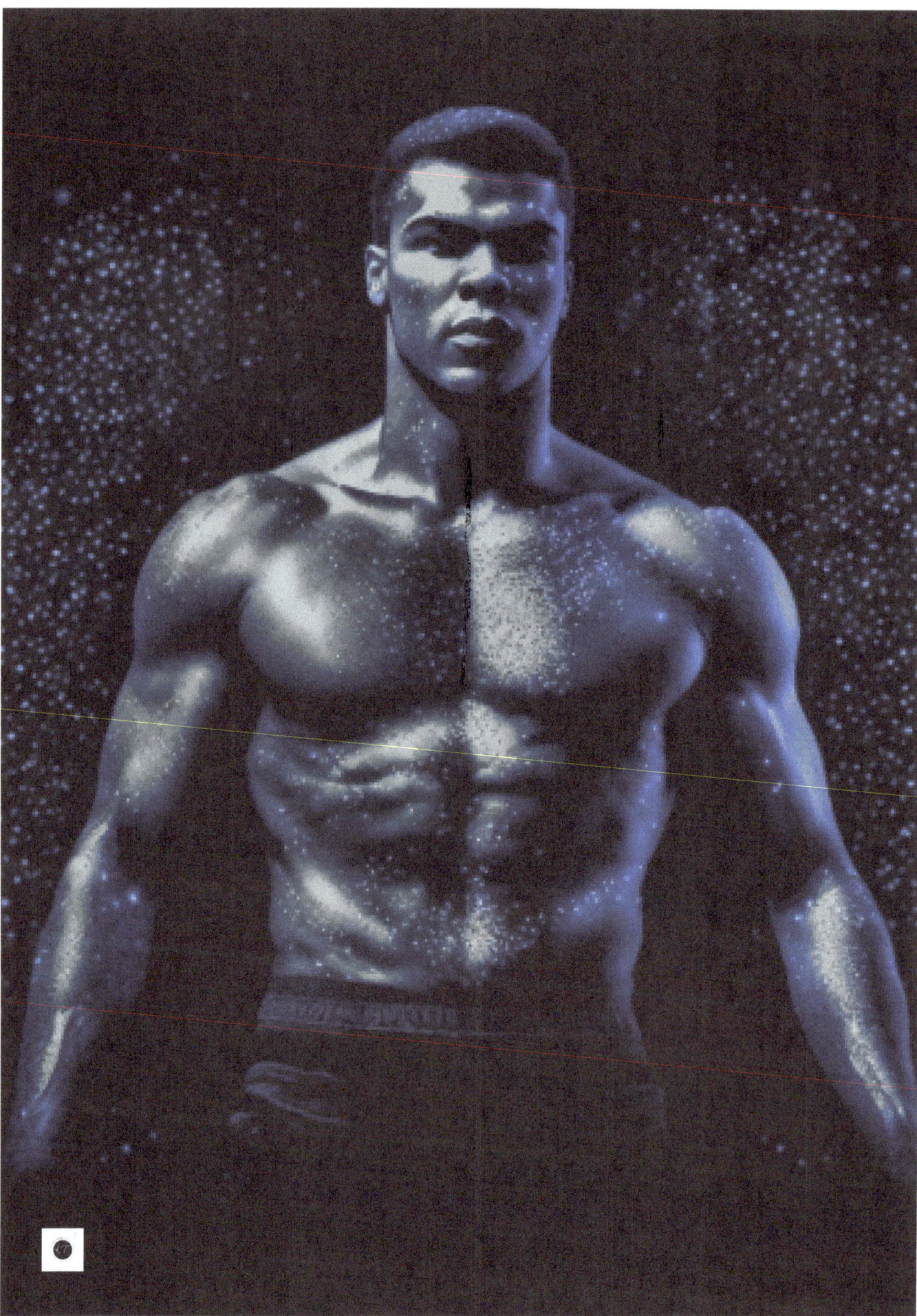

Muhammad Ali

Muhammad Ali as a singer would emphasize his charisma, ability to captivate audiences, and his extraordinary self-expression. Singing requires a combination of vocal technique, emotion, and stage presence, which aligns with Ali's talent as a boxer.

As a singer, Ali would showcase his confidence, focus, and adaptability, much like how he mesmerized audiences around the world with his exceptional boxing skills and his unforgettable personality. This role would also highlight his capacity for engaging with the public, his quick wit, and his ability to excel in high-pressure situations, as performing as a singer demands the ability to connect with the audience and deliver a powerful performance.

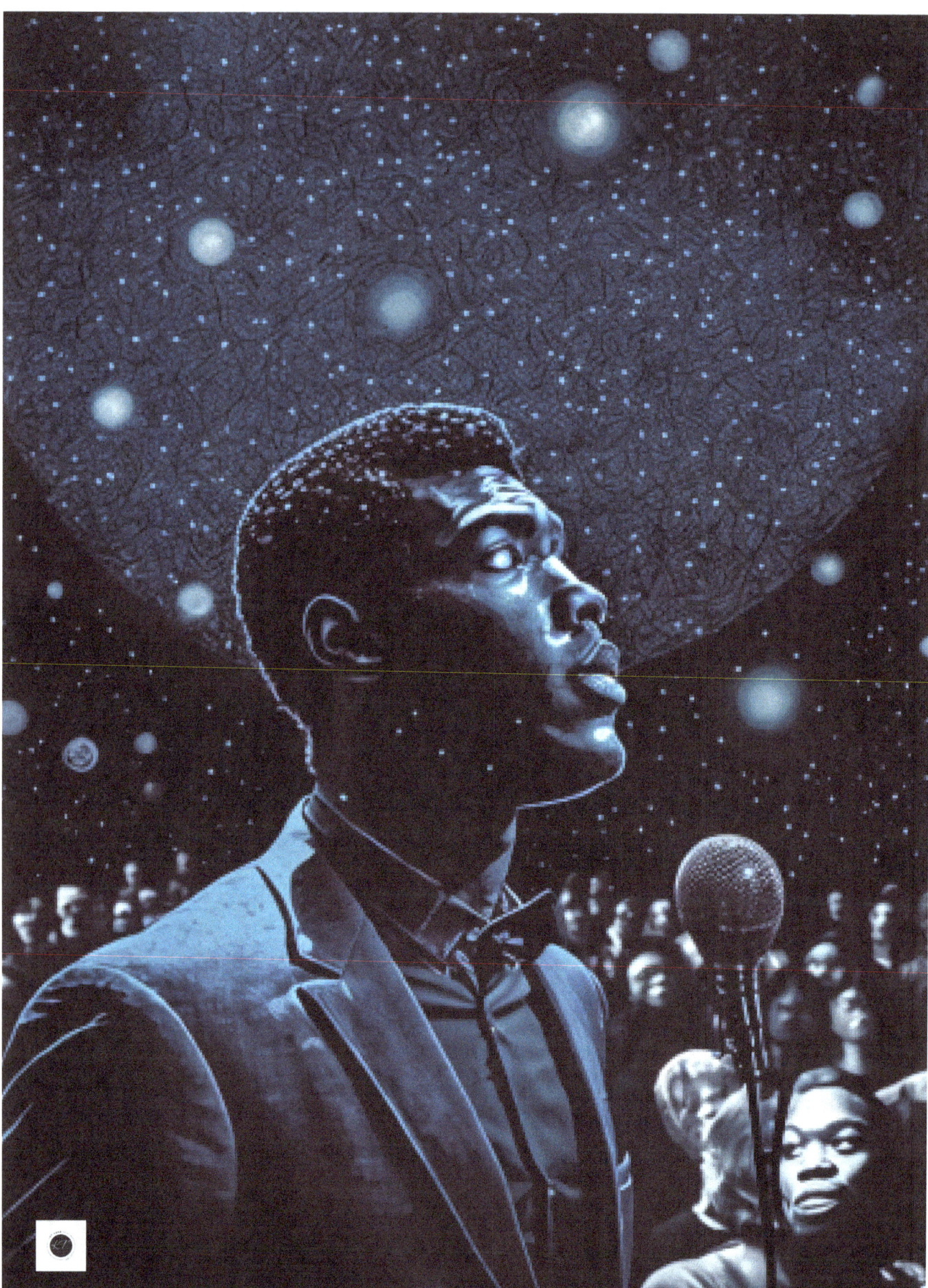

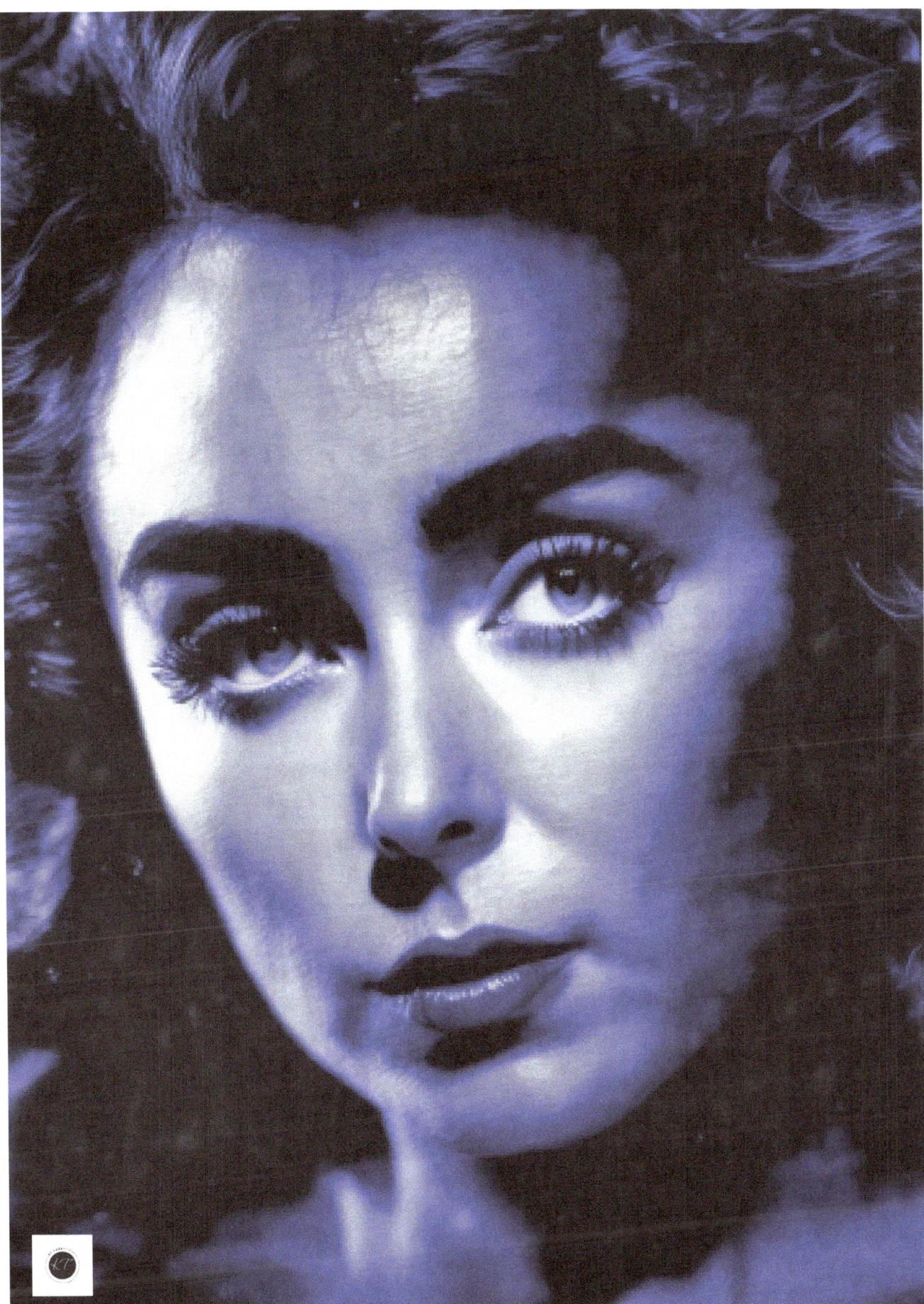

Elizabeth Taylor

Elizabeth Taylor as a figure skater, combines grace, elegance, and athleticism, which aligns with Elizabeth Taylor's glamorous image and her captivating presence on screen.

Her poise, balance, and artistic expression, much like how she mesmerized audiences with her stunning beauty and diverse acting roles, would be on display.

Figure skating is a discipline that requires both physical skill and an ability to convey emotion and tell a story through movement, reflecting the versatility and depth that characterized Taylor's career. Who wouldn't watch her skate over and over again?

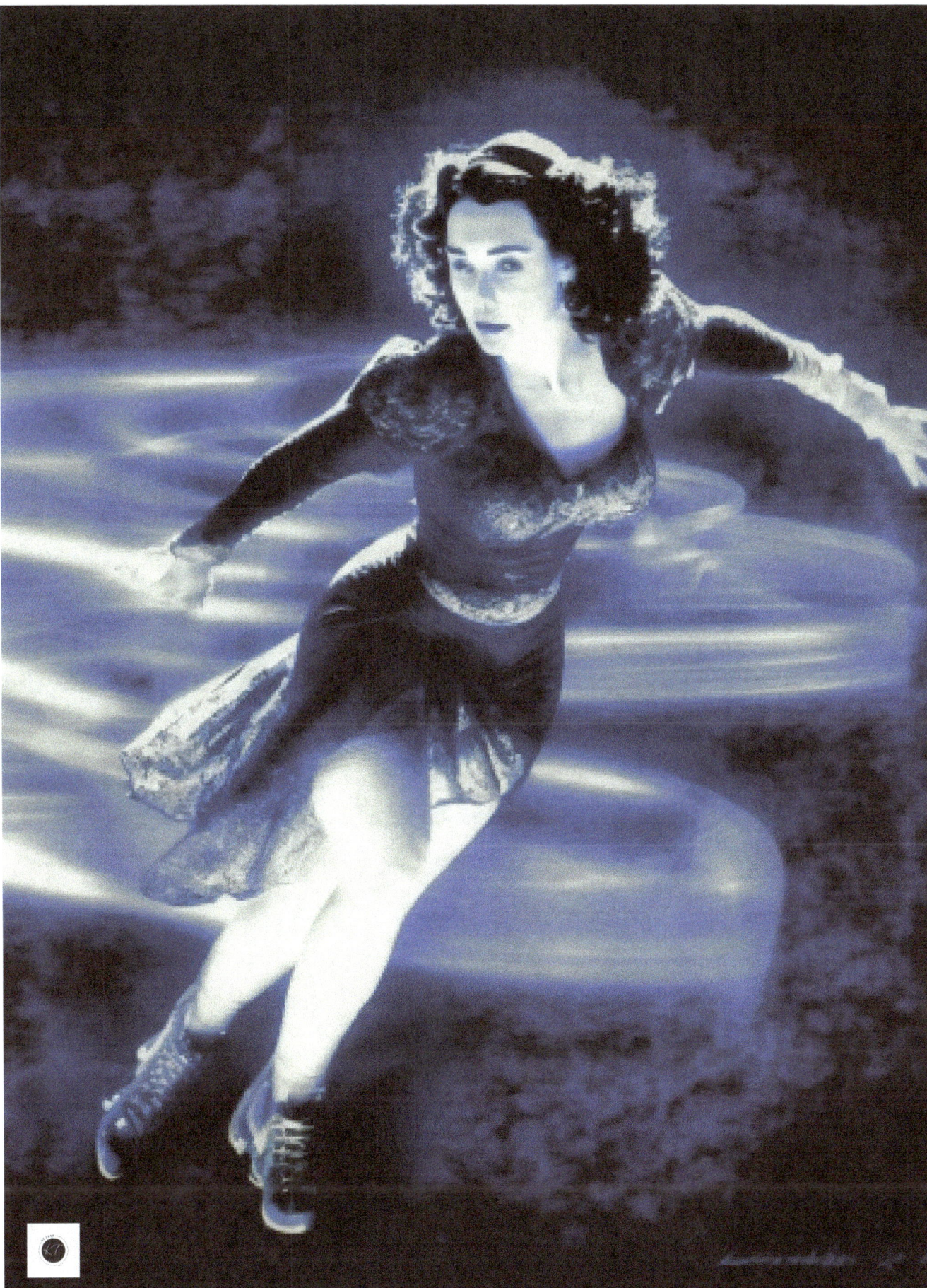

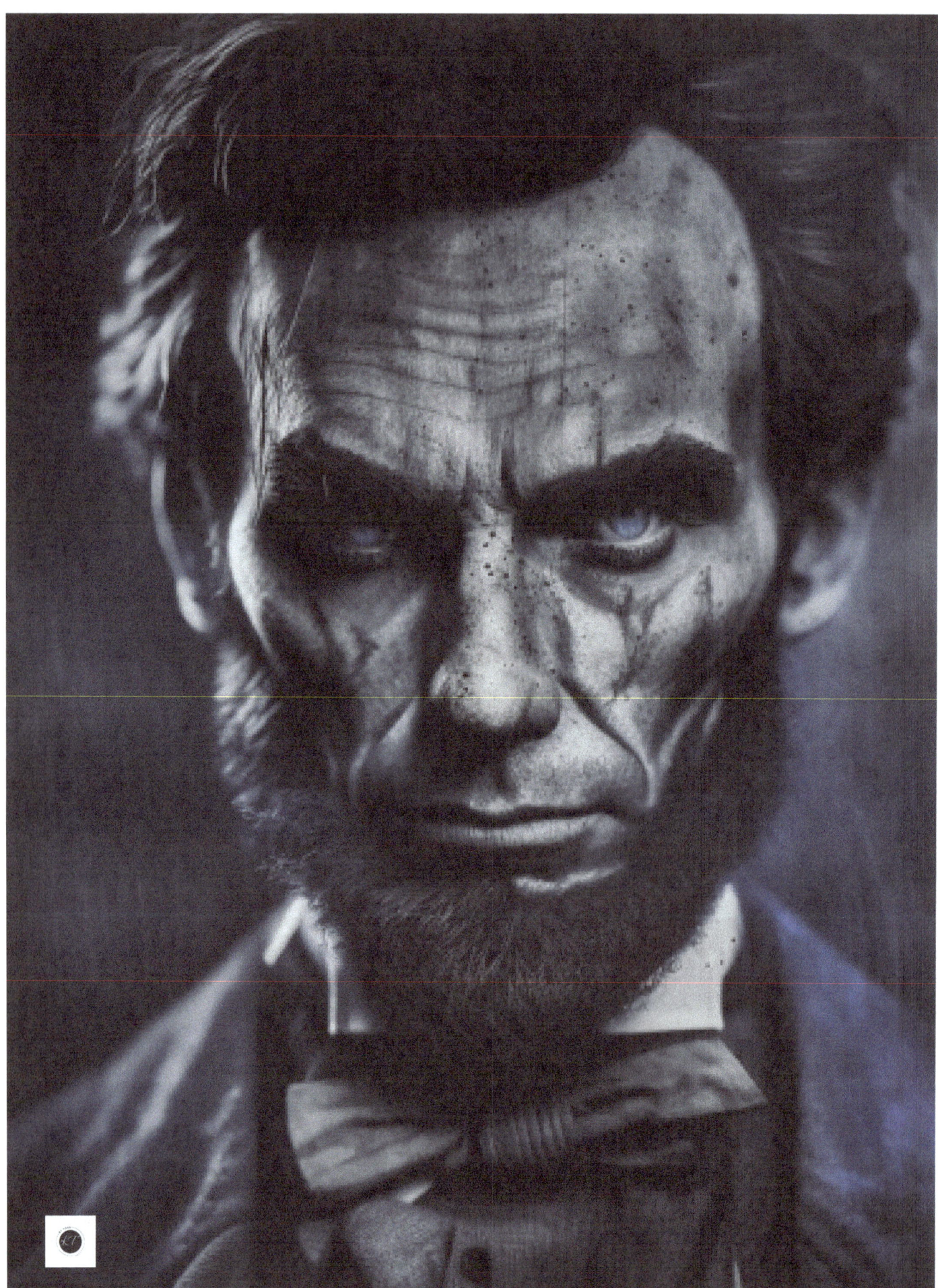

Abe Lincoln

Abraham Lincoln would fit as a wrestler. Wrestling is a sport that requires physical strength, mental resilience, and strategic thinking, which aligns well with Lincoln's strong character and leadership abilities as the 16th President of the United States.
Additionally, wrestling is an individual sport with a strong emphasis on personal honor and integrity, reflecting Lincoln's commitment to principles and his reputation for honesty.

It is worth mentioning that Lincoln was known to have participated in wrestling matches in his youth, which further solidifies the connection between the sport and his persona. I know he looks like the Joker, but hey, at least there's no axe in his hand!

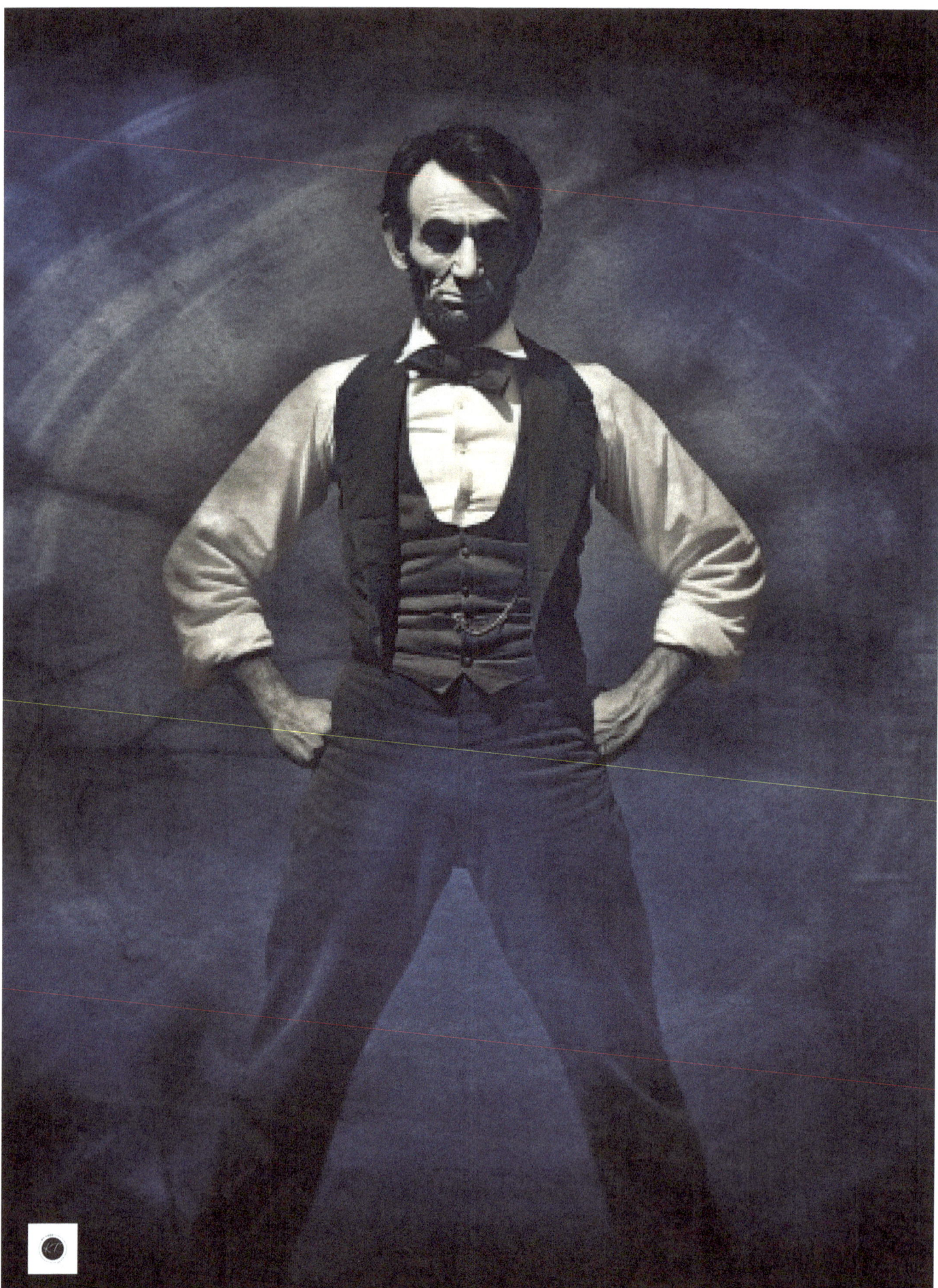

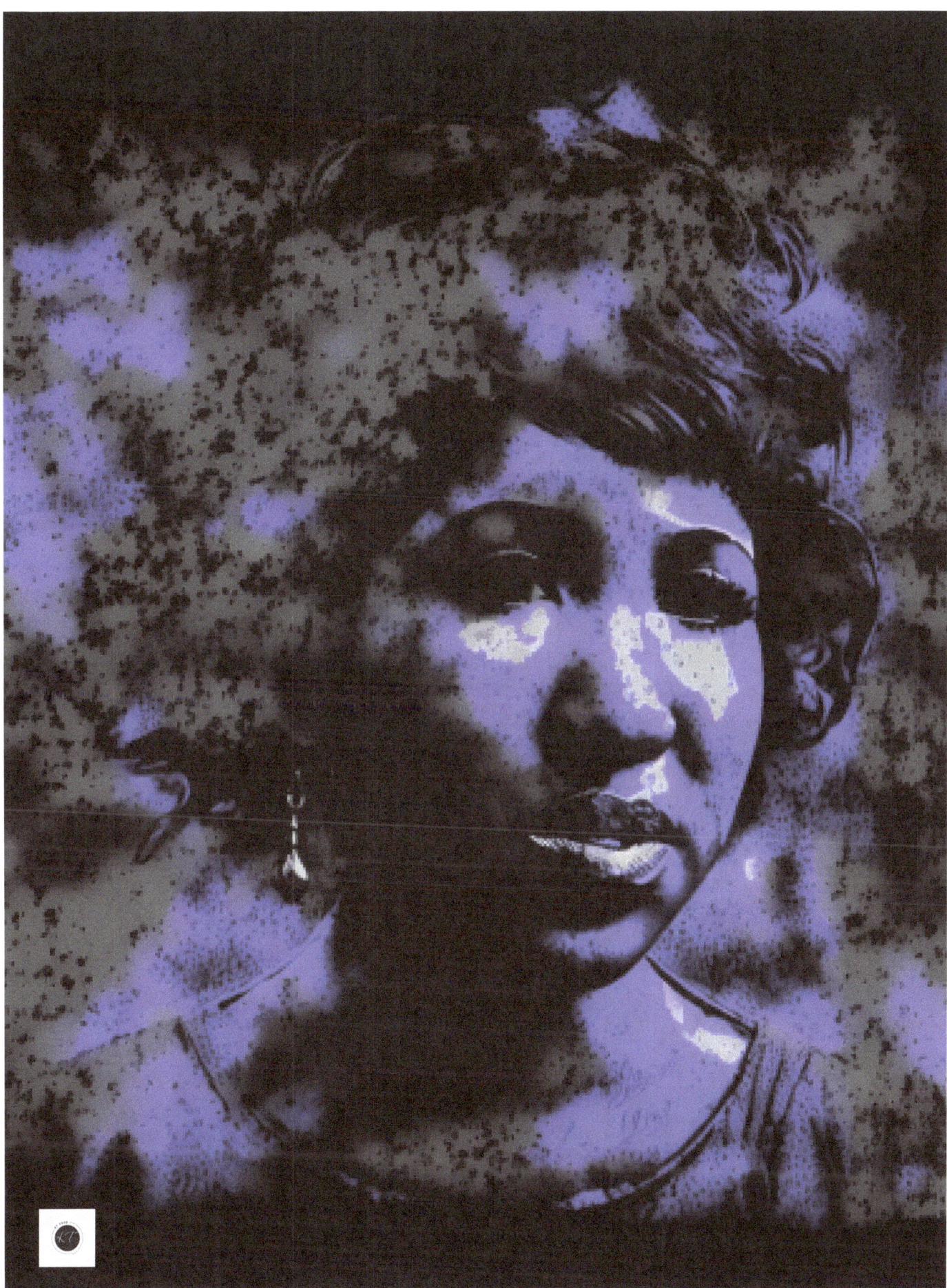

Aretha Franklin

Aretha Franklin as a volleyball player requires teamwork, coordination, and a strong sense of rhythm and timing, which aligns with Aretha's talent as a singer and her ability to connect with audiences through her powerful and soulful voice.

Aretha could be imagined as a setter or an outside hitter, positions that require excellent communication skills, agility, and the ability to make decisive plays. These roles would showcase her leadership qualities and her ability to adapt and excel in various situations, much like her diverse musical career.

Yes, volleyball, even coming from Detroit, respect that! R_E_S_P_E_C_T!

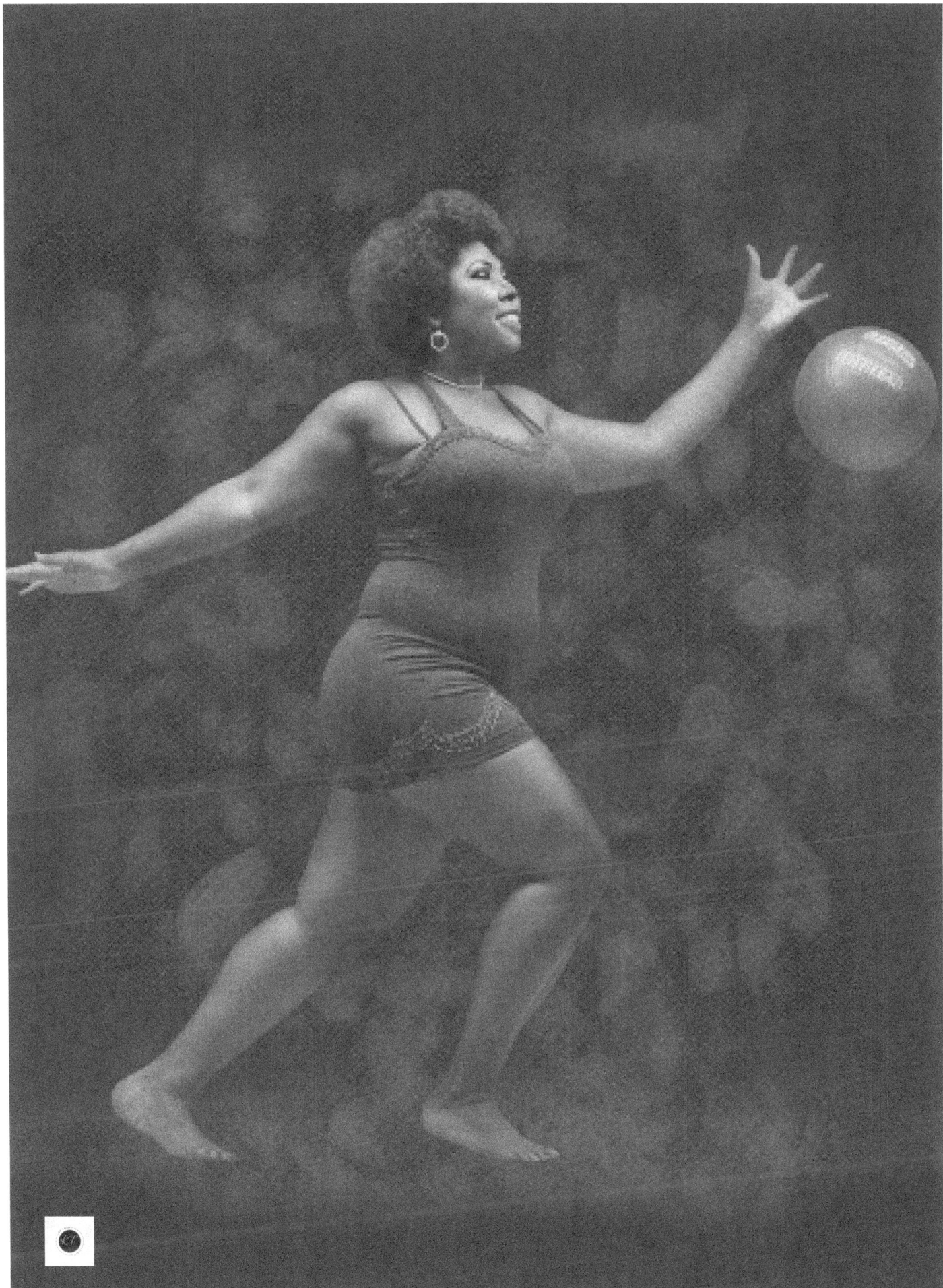

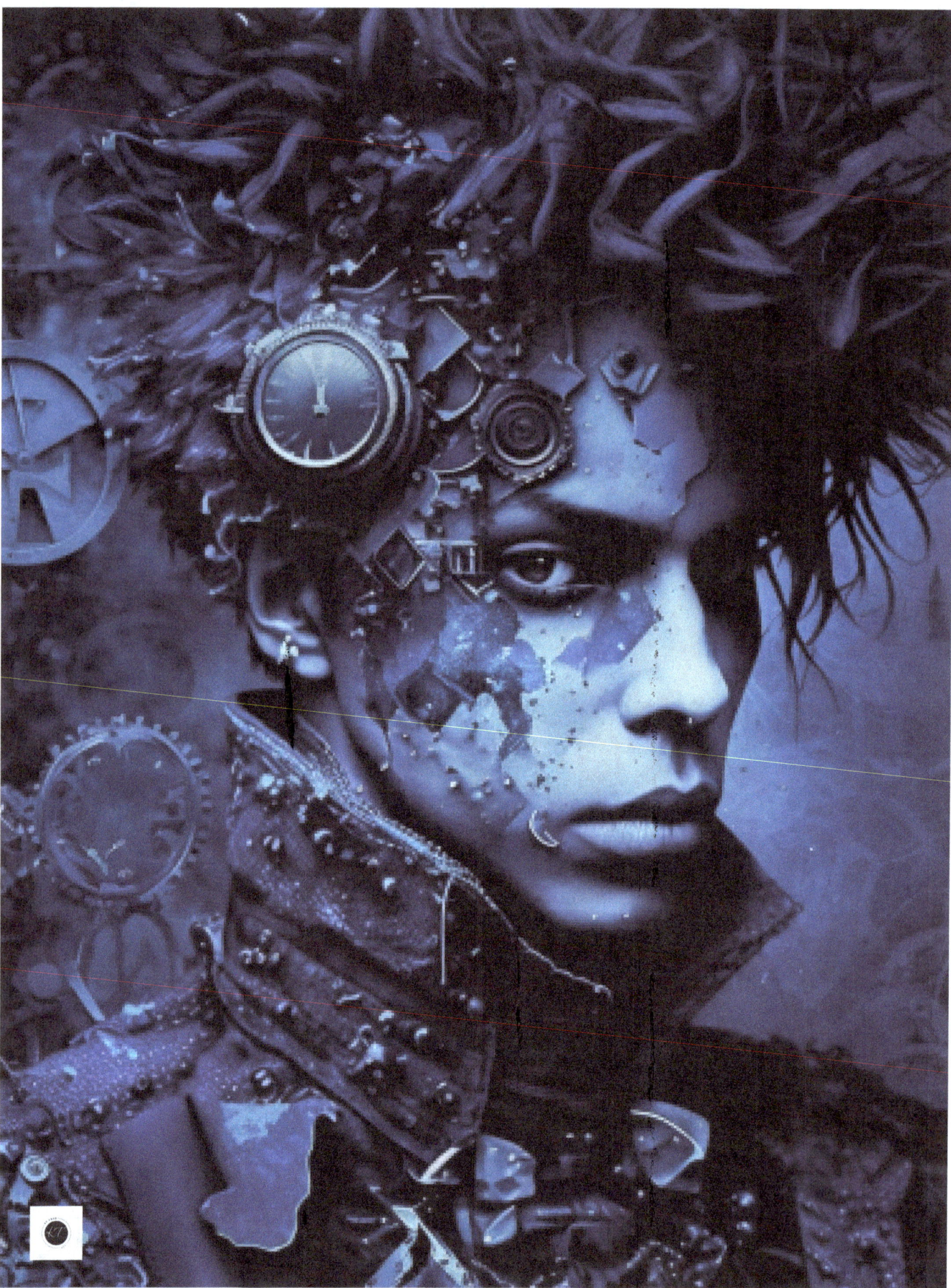

Prince

Prince as a basketball player would emphasize his agility, precision, and ability to captivate audiences with his incredible performances. Basketball is a sport that requires a combination of speed, coordination, and teamwork, which aligns with Prince's talent as a singer, multi-instrumentalist, and performer and band leader.

As a baller, Prince would showcase his quick reflexes, focus, and adaptability, much like how he mesmerized audiences around the world with his music and unforgettable stage presence. This role would also highlight his capacity for concentration, his competitiveness, as basketball games can be fast-paced and intense.

In fact, Prince was known to be a fan of basketball and played the sport in high school, making this portrayal particularly fitting. Even if he plays in a blouse!

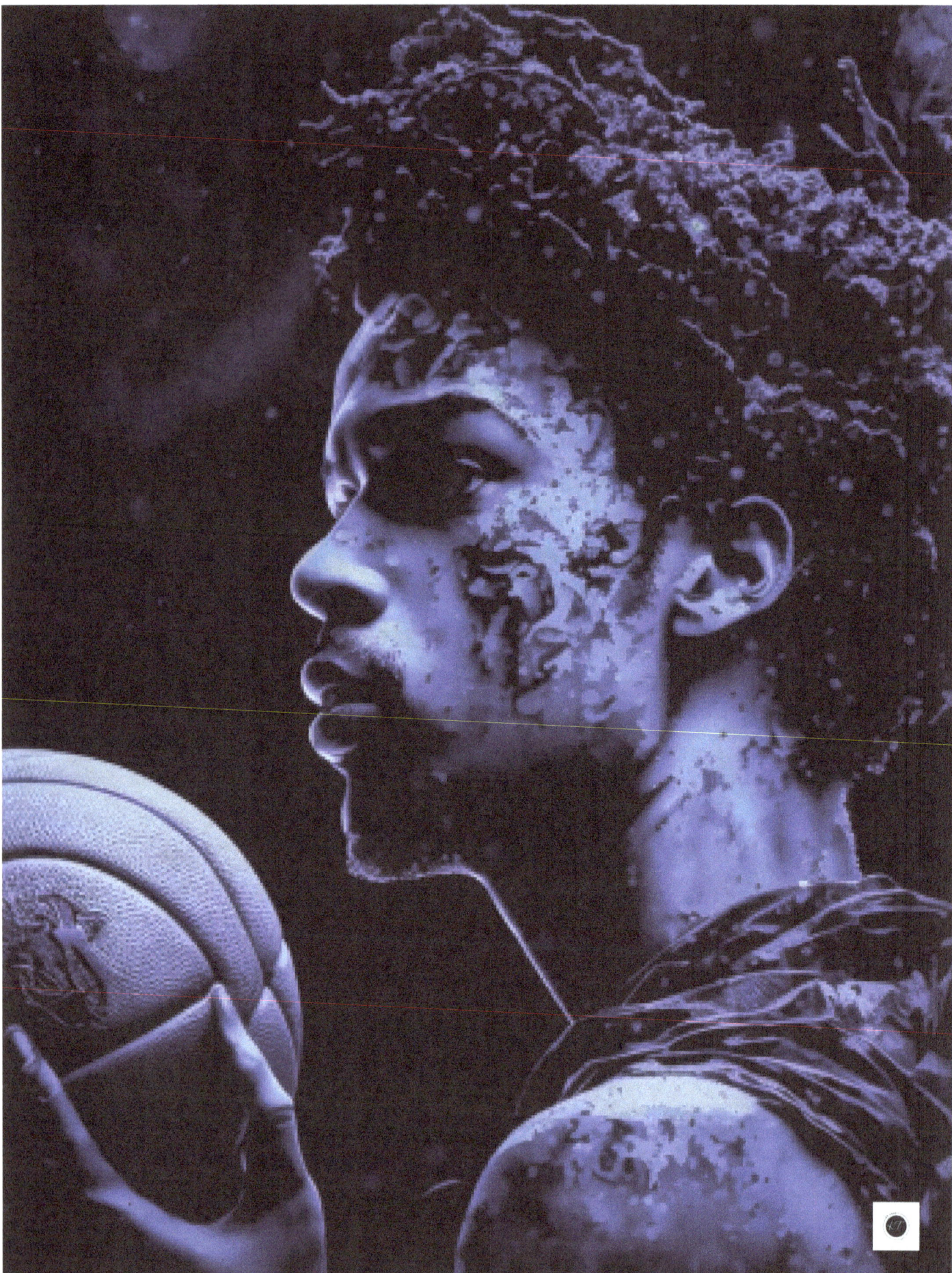

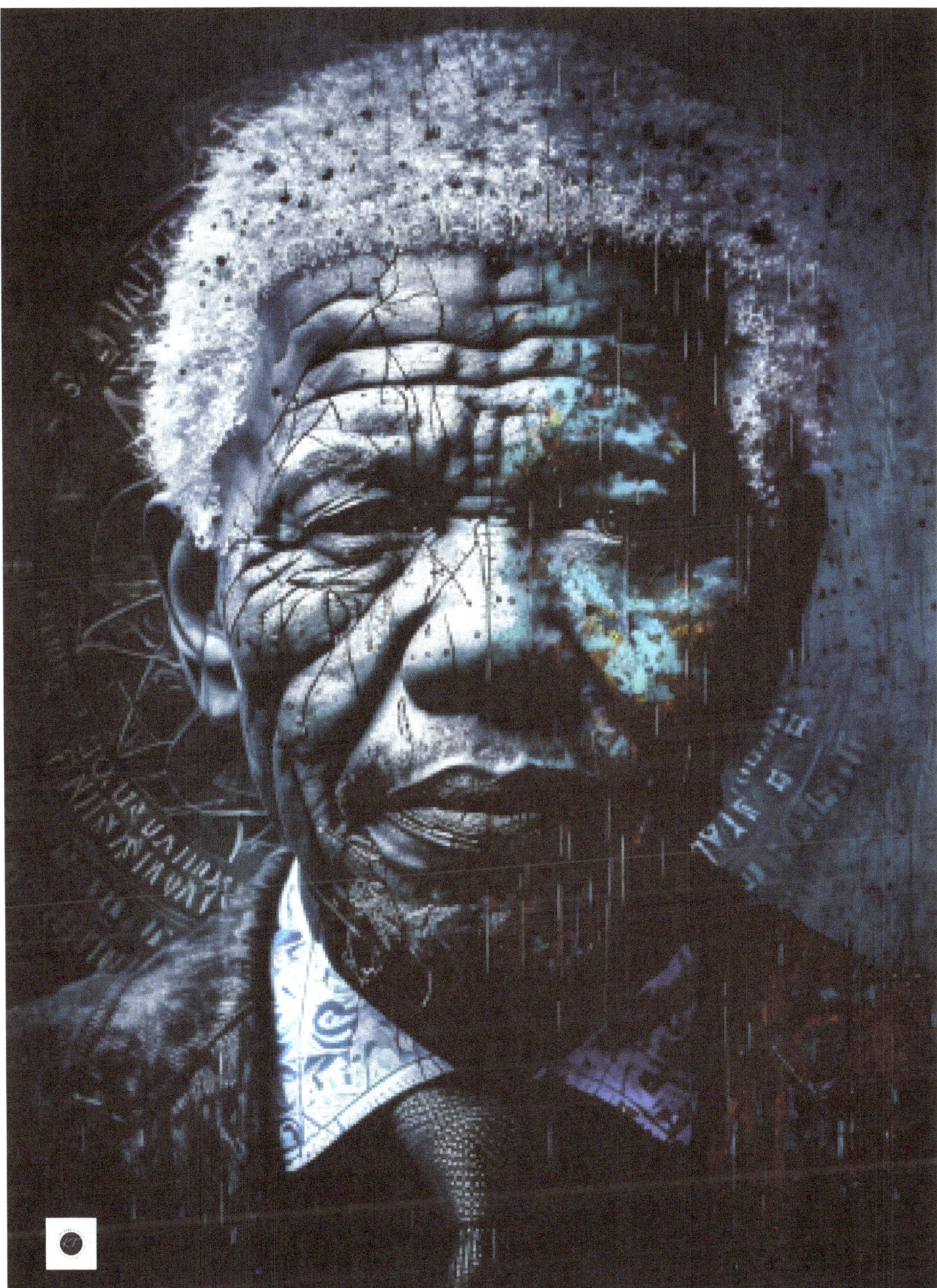

Nelson Mandela

Nelson Mandela as a rugby player would emphasize his unifying spirit, resilience, and ability to inspire and captivate audiences through his leadership and vision for a more equitable society.

Rugby requires a combination of strength, teamwork, and strategic thinking, which aligns with Mandela's talent as a political leader and his iconic status as a symbol of hope, forgiveness, and unity in post-apartheid South Africa. Twenty-seven years...no words.

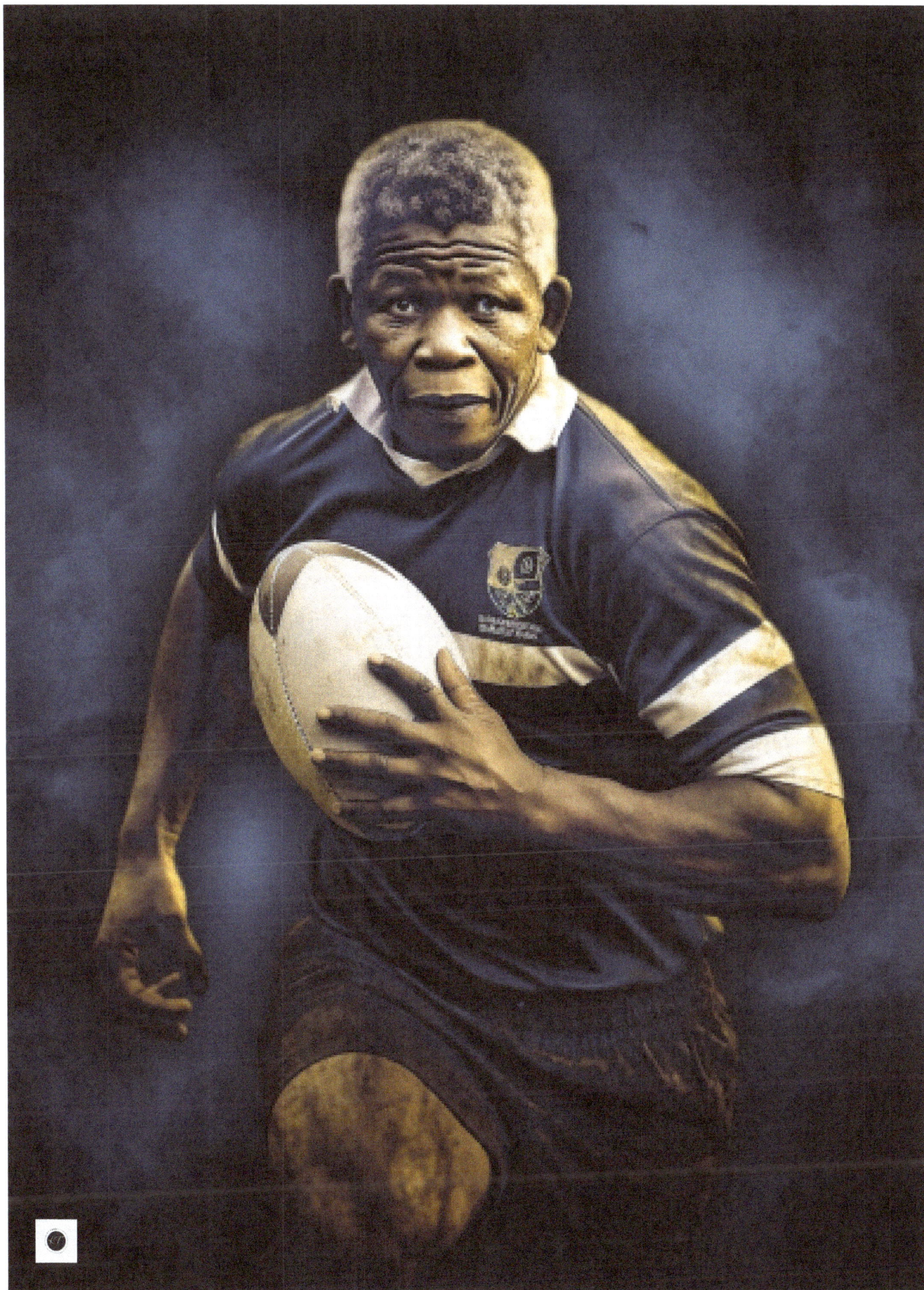

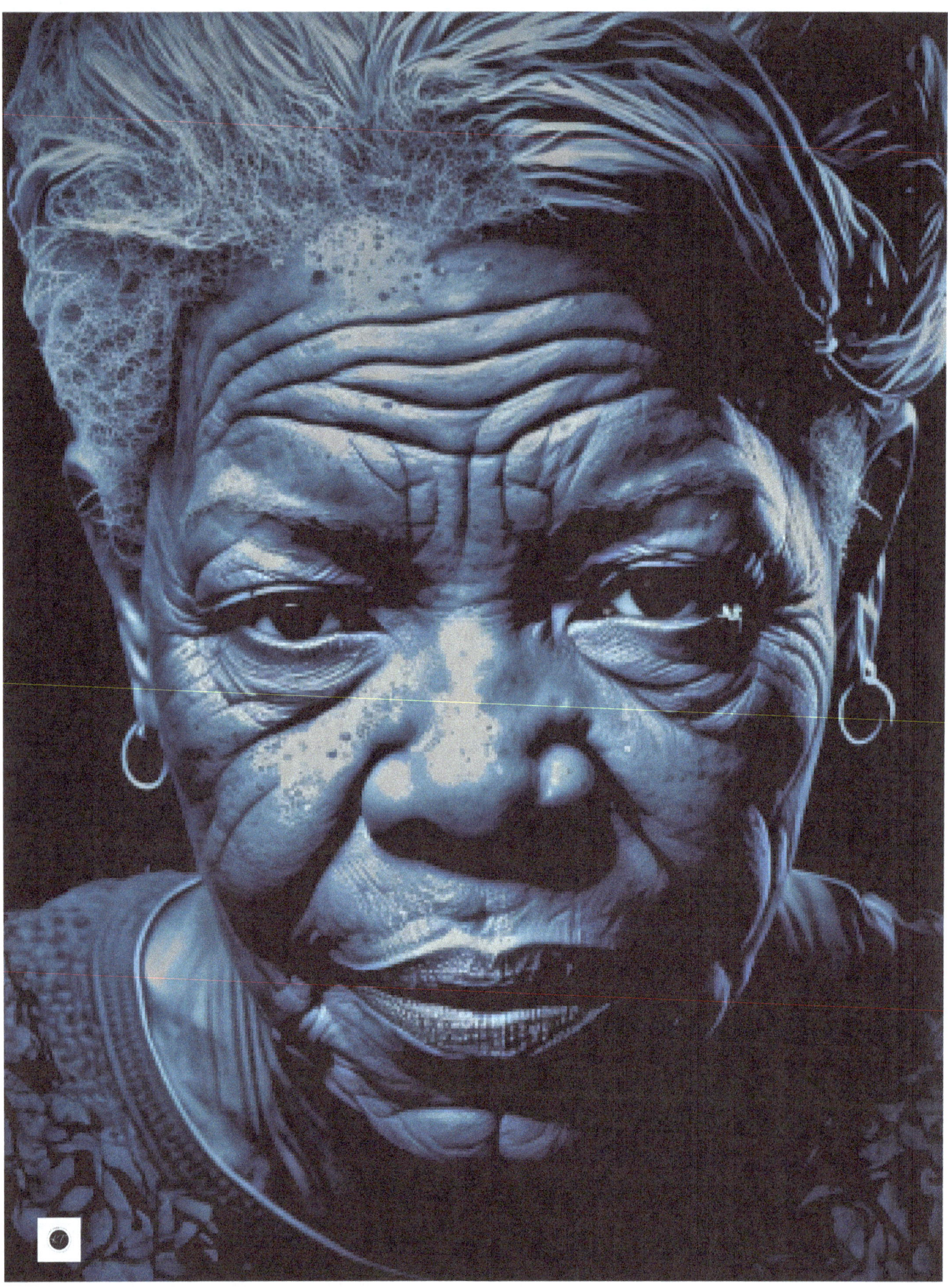

Maya Angelou

Maya Angelou as a swimmer would emphasize her resilience, grace, and ability to inspire and captivate audiences through her powerful words and storytelling. Swimming requires a combination of skill, endurance, and poise, which aligns with Angelou's talent as a writer, poet, and civil rights activist and her status as a champion of strength, courage, and wisdom.

As a swimmer, Maya Angelou would showcase her determination, focus, and ability to overcome challenges with grace and perseverance, much like how she navigated the complex world of literature and activism with her captivating prose and unwavering commitment to social justice. And, you'd better make a good first impression!

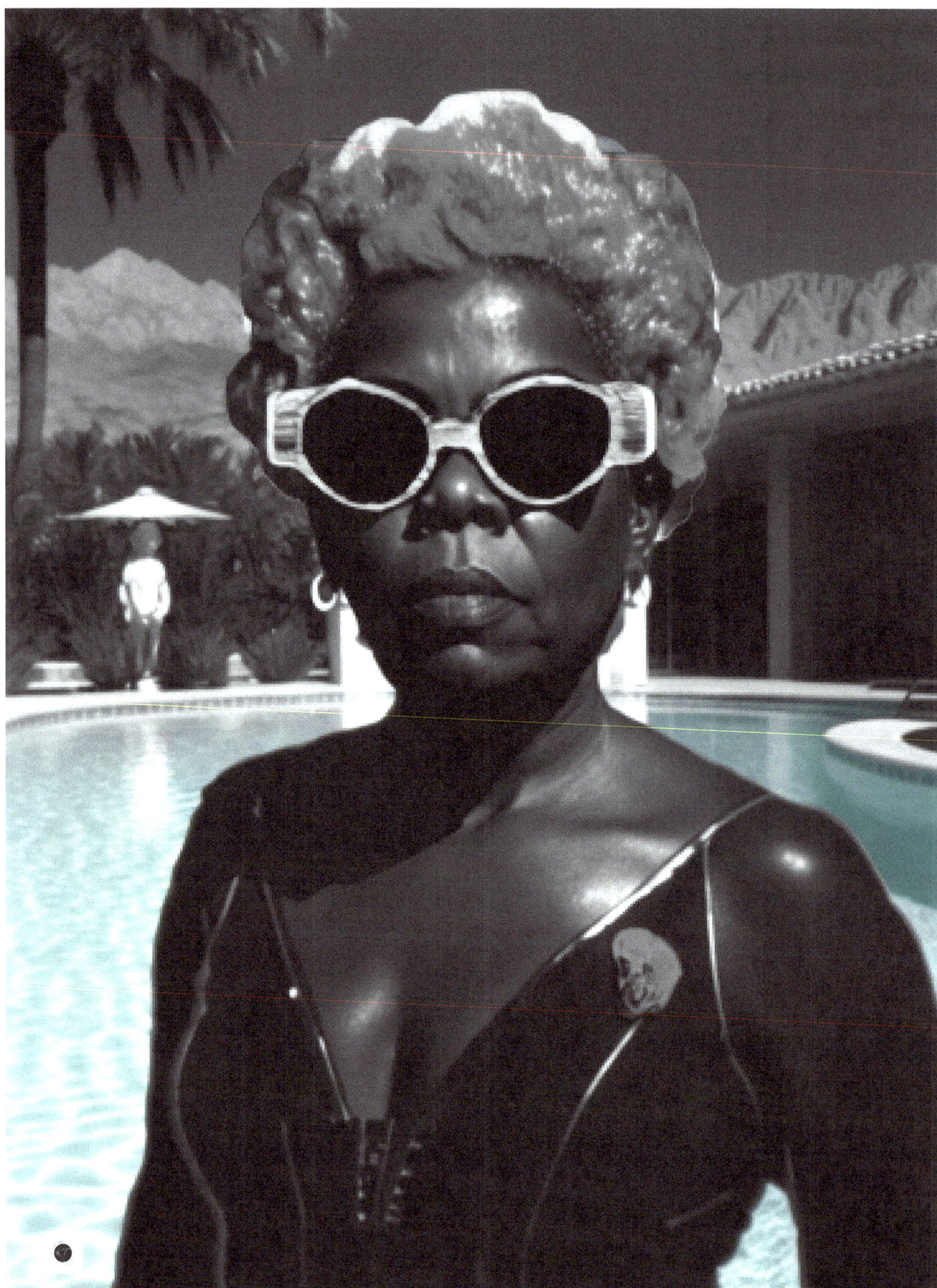

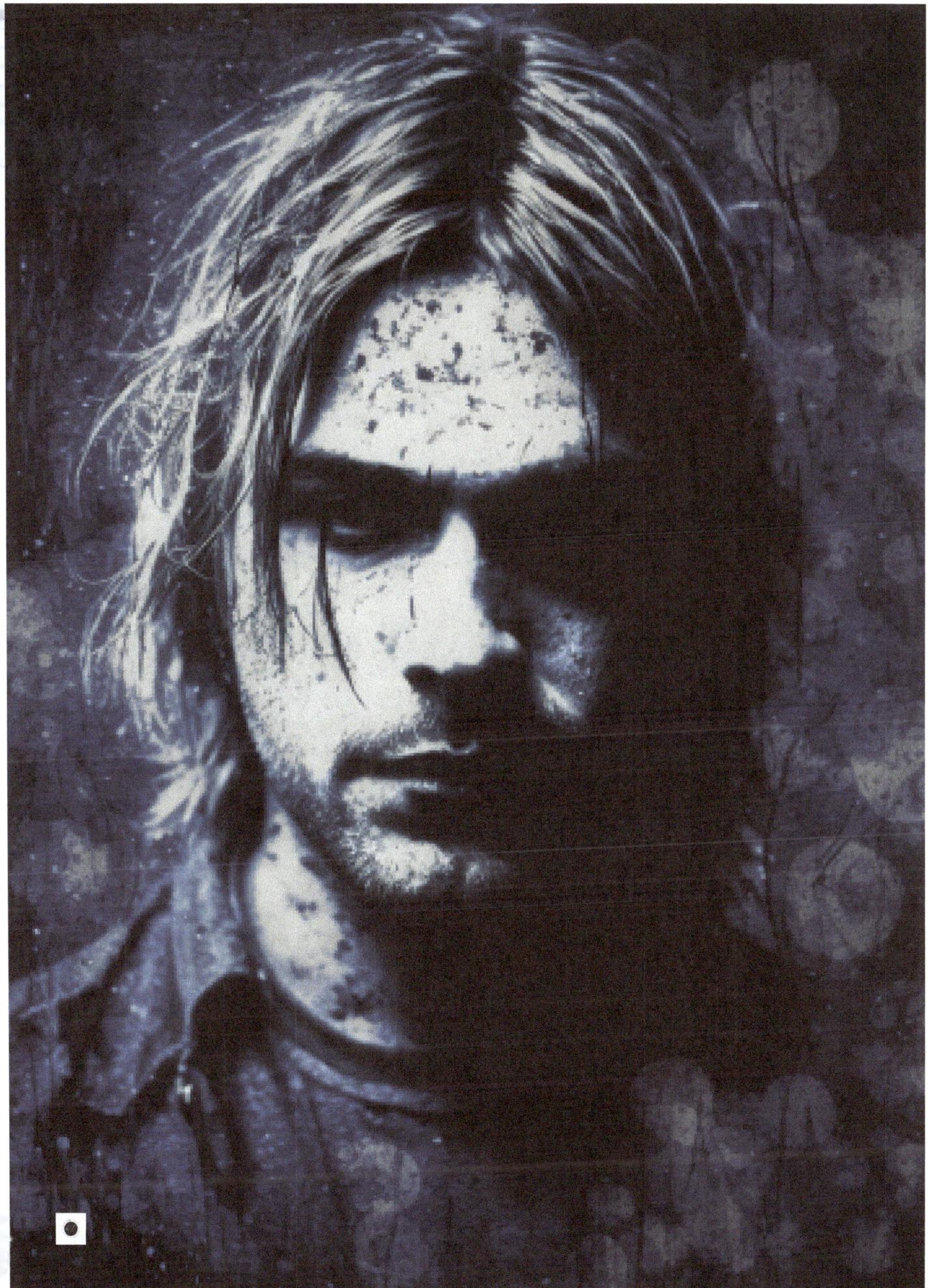

Kurt Cobain

Kurt Cobain as a skateboarder would emphasize his rebellious spirit, creativity, and ability to connect with audiences through his authentic expression. Skateboarding requires a combination of skill, individuality, and adaptability, which aligns with Cobain's talent as a musician and the grunge movement and counterculture.

As a skateboarder, Kurt Cobain would showcase his unique perspectives, much like how he revolutionized the world of music with his sound and his commitment to artistic integrity. This role would also highlight his capacity for pushing boundaries, and his drive for self-expression, as skateboarding demands a high level of skill, creativity, and personal style. Courtney Love would be right next to him.

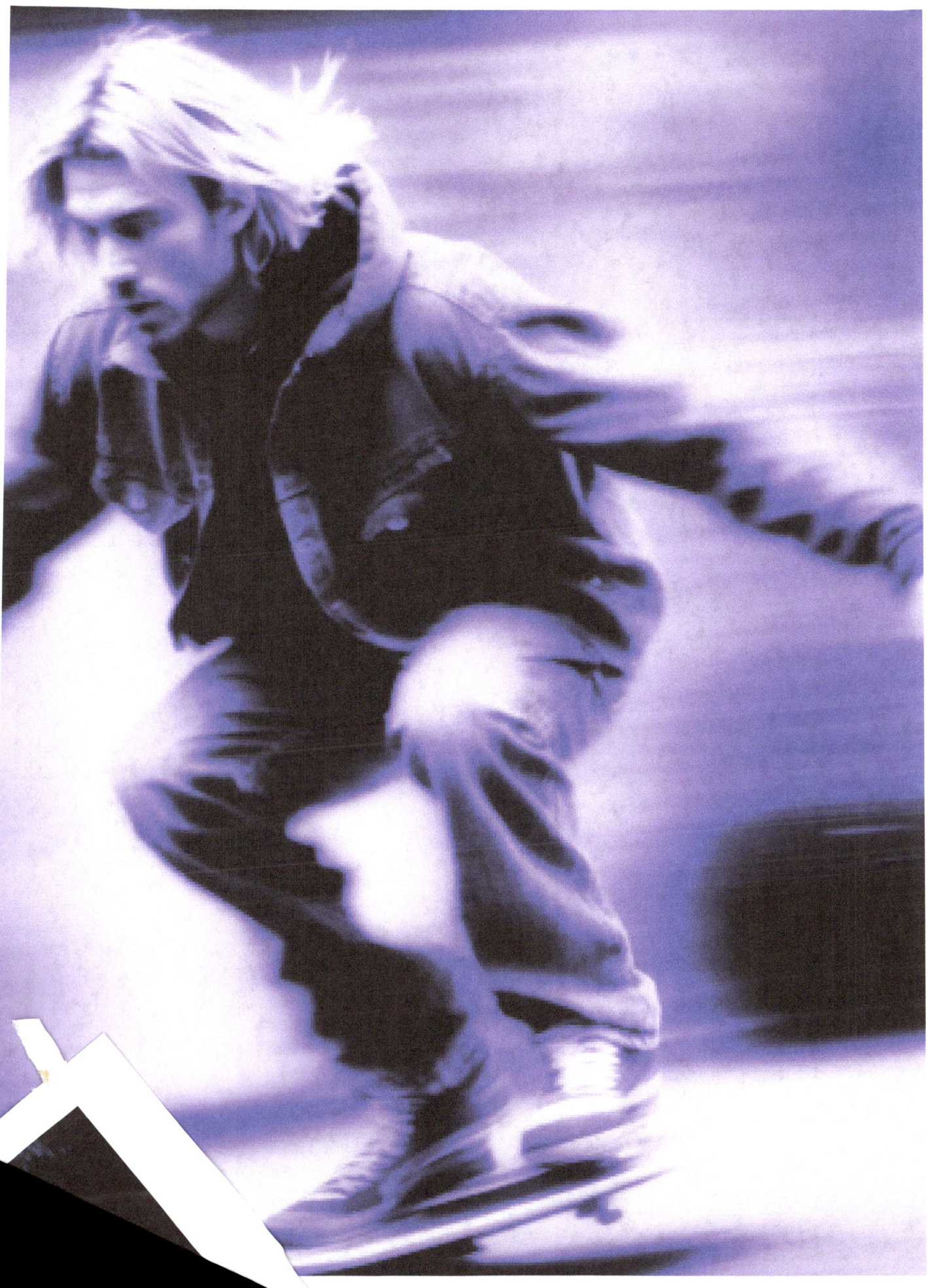

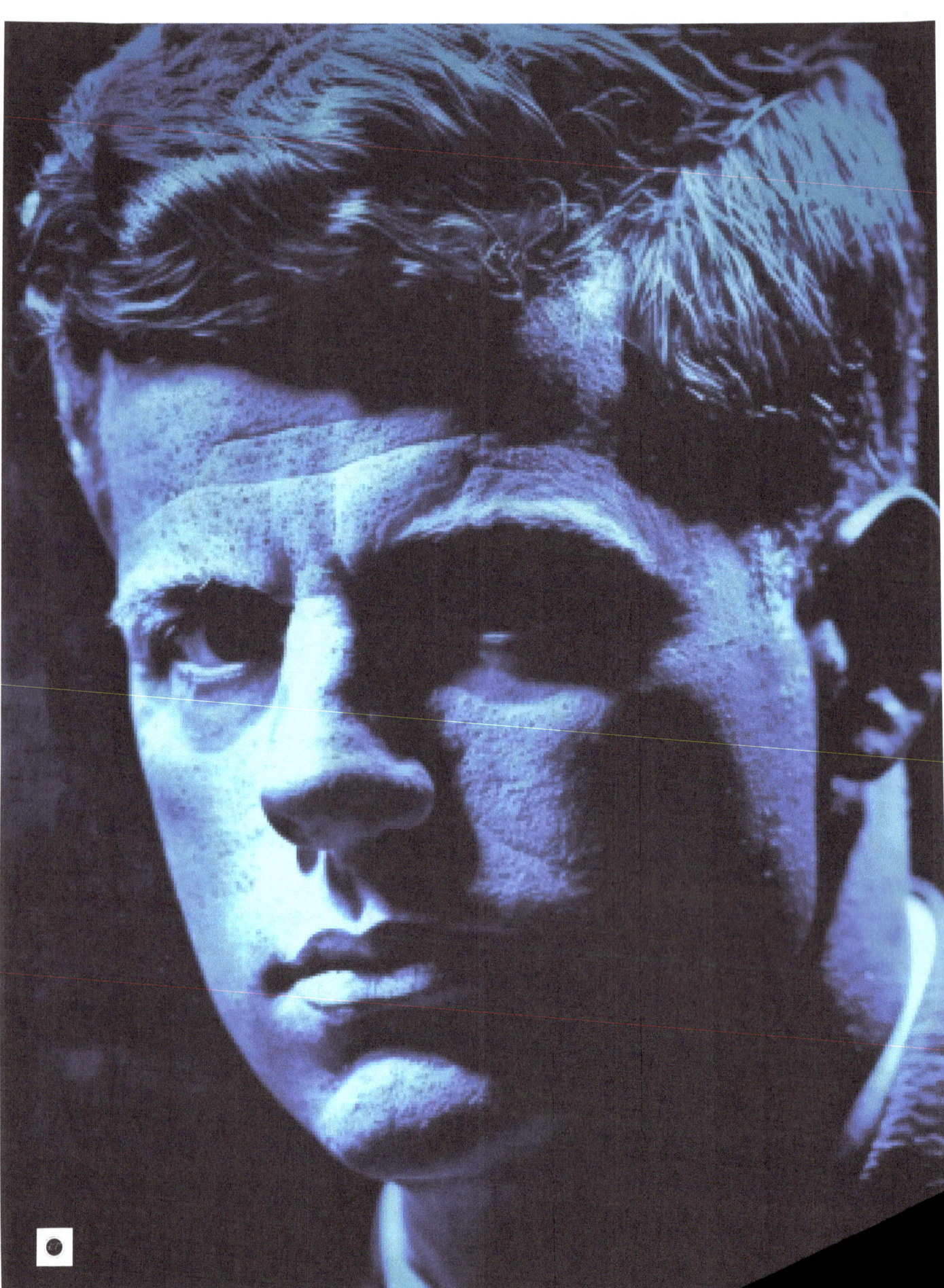

John F. Kennedy

JFK as a speed boat racer would emphasize his charismatic spirit, love for adventure, and ability to inspire and captivate audiences.

Speed boat racing is a sport that requires a combination of skill, fearlessness, and quick thinking, which aligns with JFK's talent as a political leader and his iconic status as a representative of a new, optimistic era in American history.

As a speed boat racer, JFK would showcase his determination, focus, and ability to approach challenges with confidence, much like how he navigated the complex world of politics with his charm and unwavering commitment to progress.

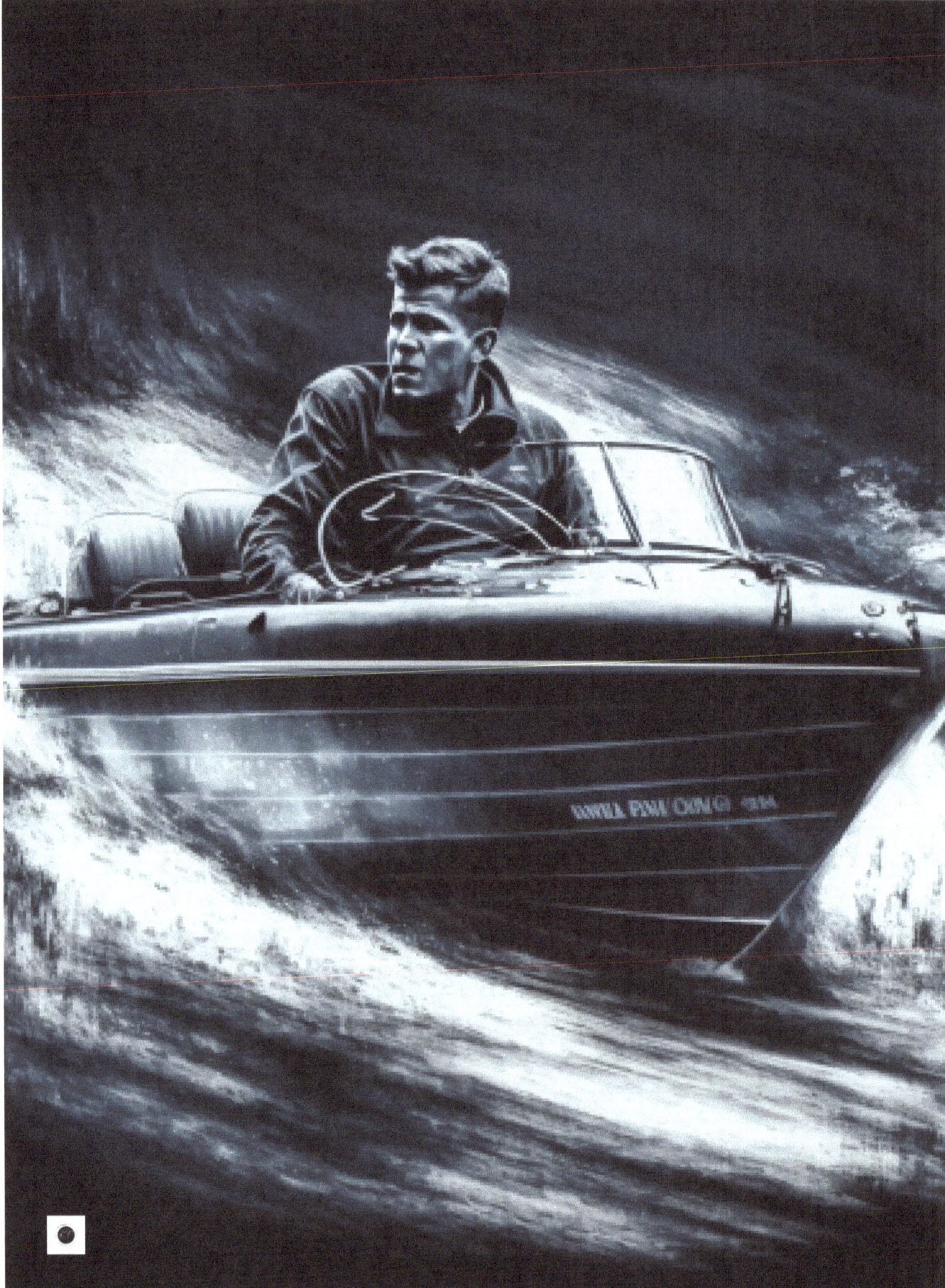

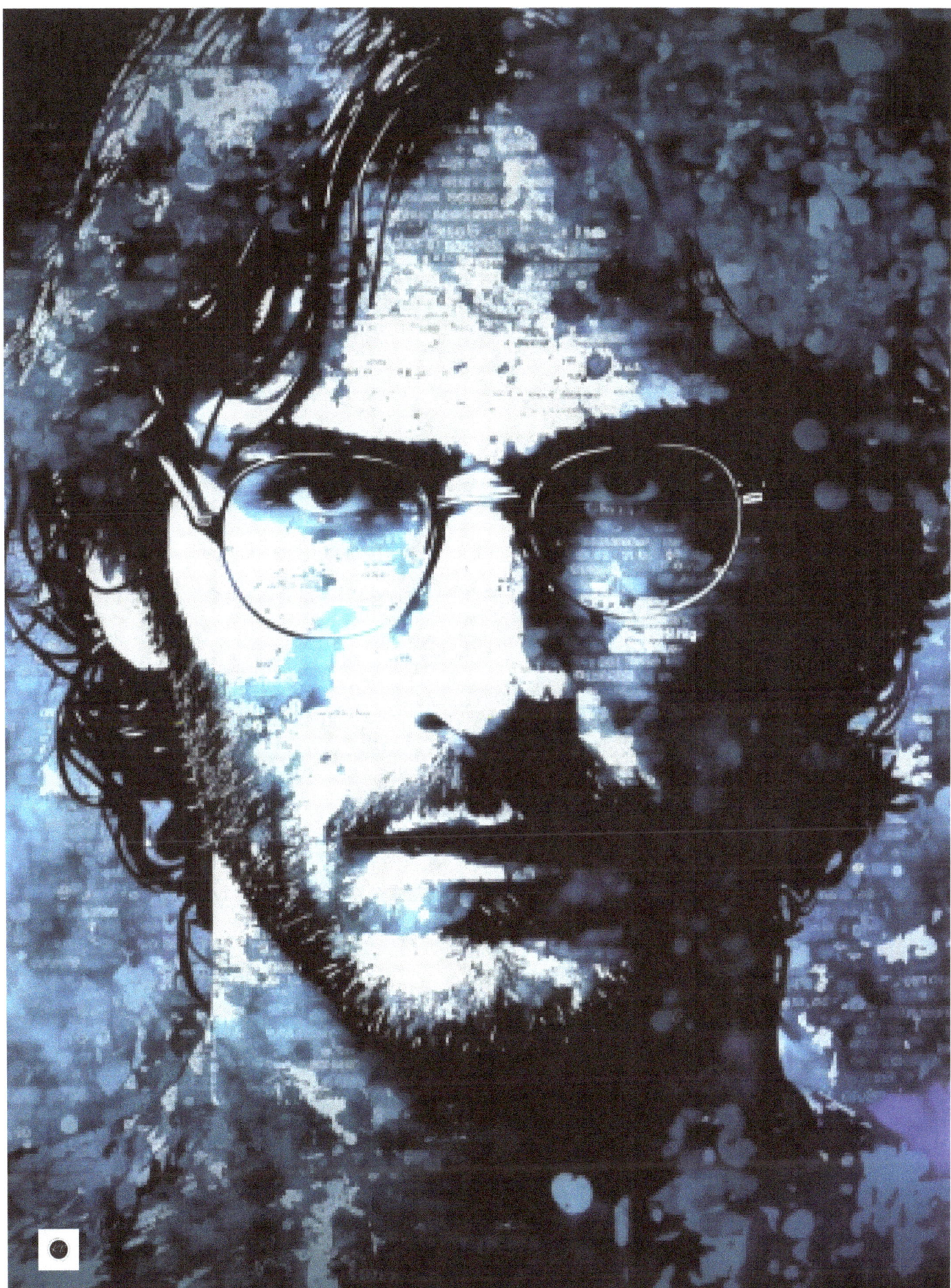

Steve Jobs

Steve Jobs as a Frisbee golf player would emphasize his inventive spirit, precision, and ability to think outside the box. Frisbee golf, also known as disc golf, irequires a combination of skill, strategy, and adaptability, which aligns with Jobs' talent in the technology industry.

As a Frisbee golf player, Steve Jobs would showcase his determination, focus, and ability to approach challenges with a unique perspective, much like how he revolutionized the world of technology with his innovative products and his unwavering pursuit of excellence. We'd probably have flying cars if he were still around.

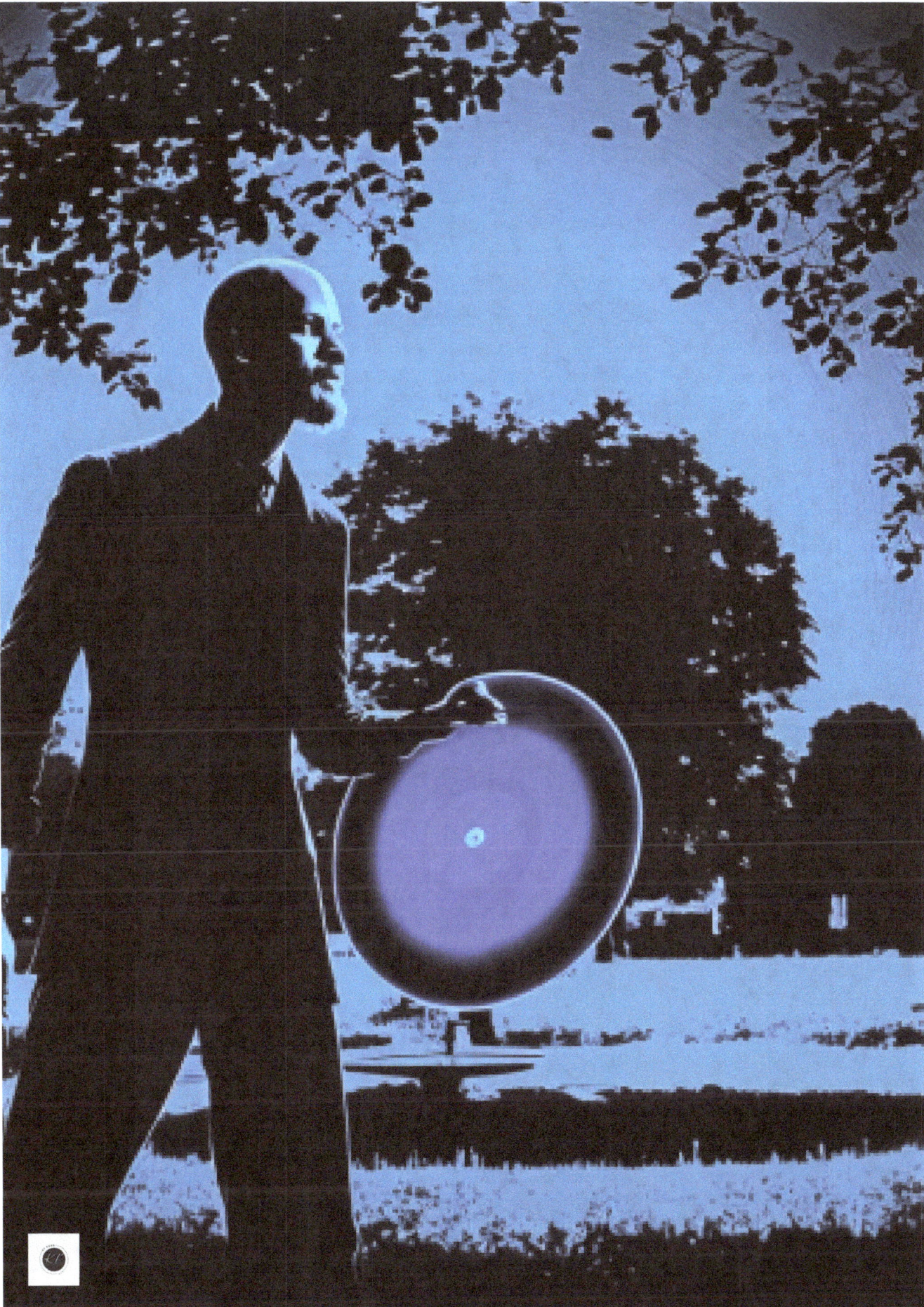

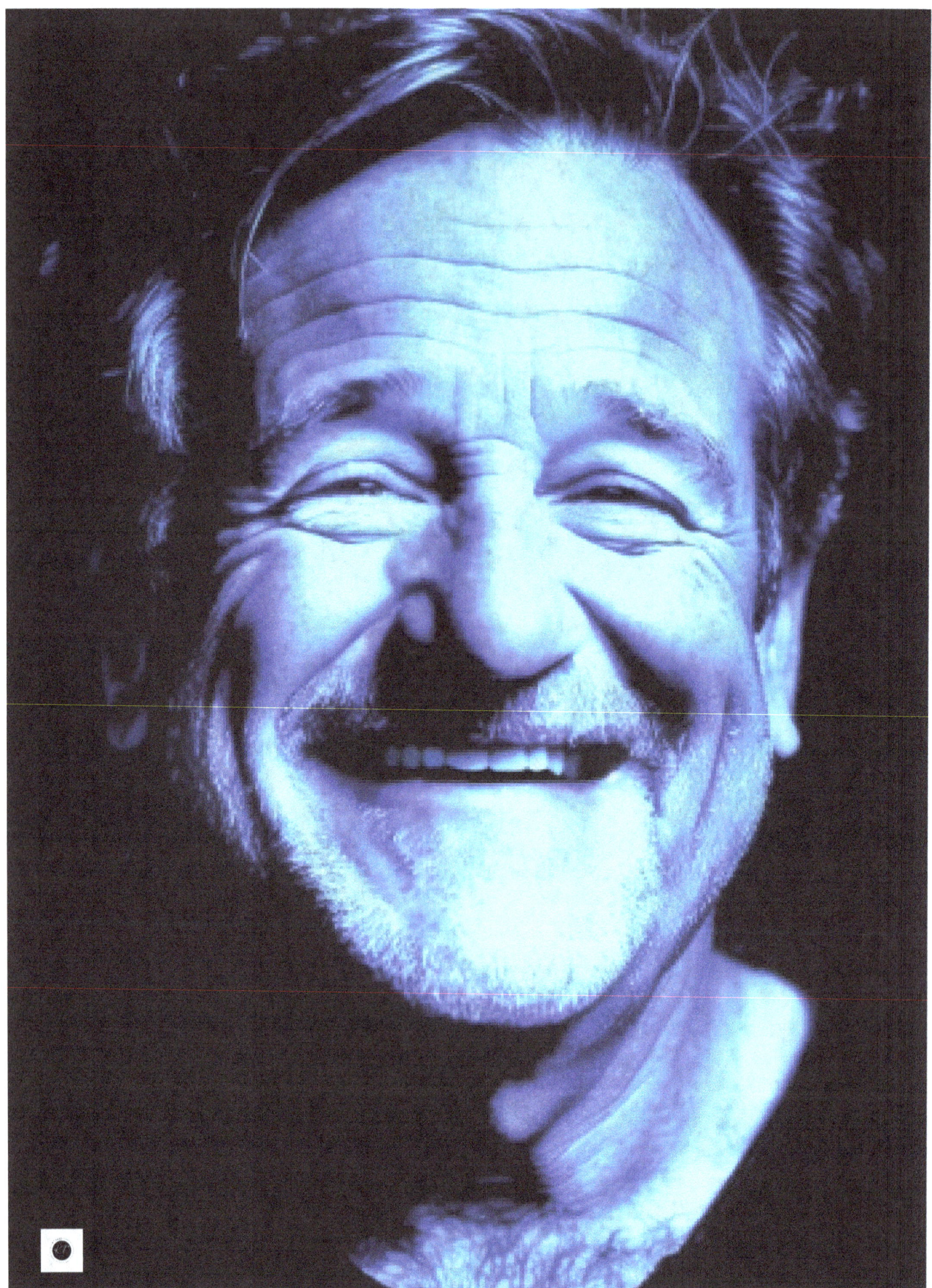

Robin Williams

Fencing would be an intriguing choice for Robin Williams as it is a sport that combines physical agility, strategic thinking, and a touch of theatrical flair. These qualities align with Williams' energetic and versatile performances, as well as his ability to captivate audiences with his humor and improvisational skills.

As a fencer, Williams would showcase his quick reflexes, wit, and adaptability, much like how he engaged audiences with his rapid-fire comedy and diverse acting roles. Fencing is often considered an art form as well as a sport, reflecting the creativity and expressiveness that characterized Williams' career.

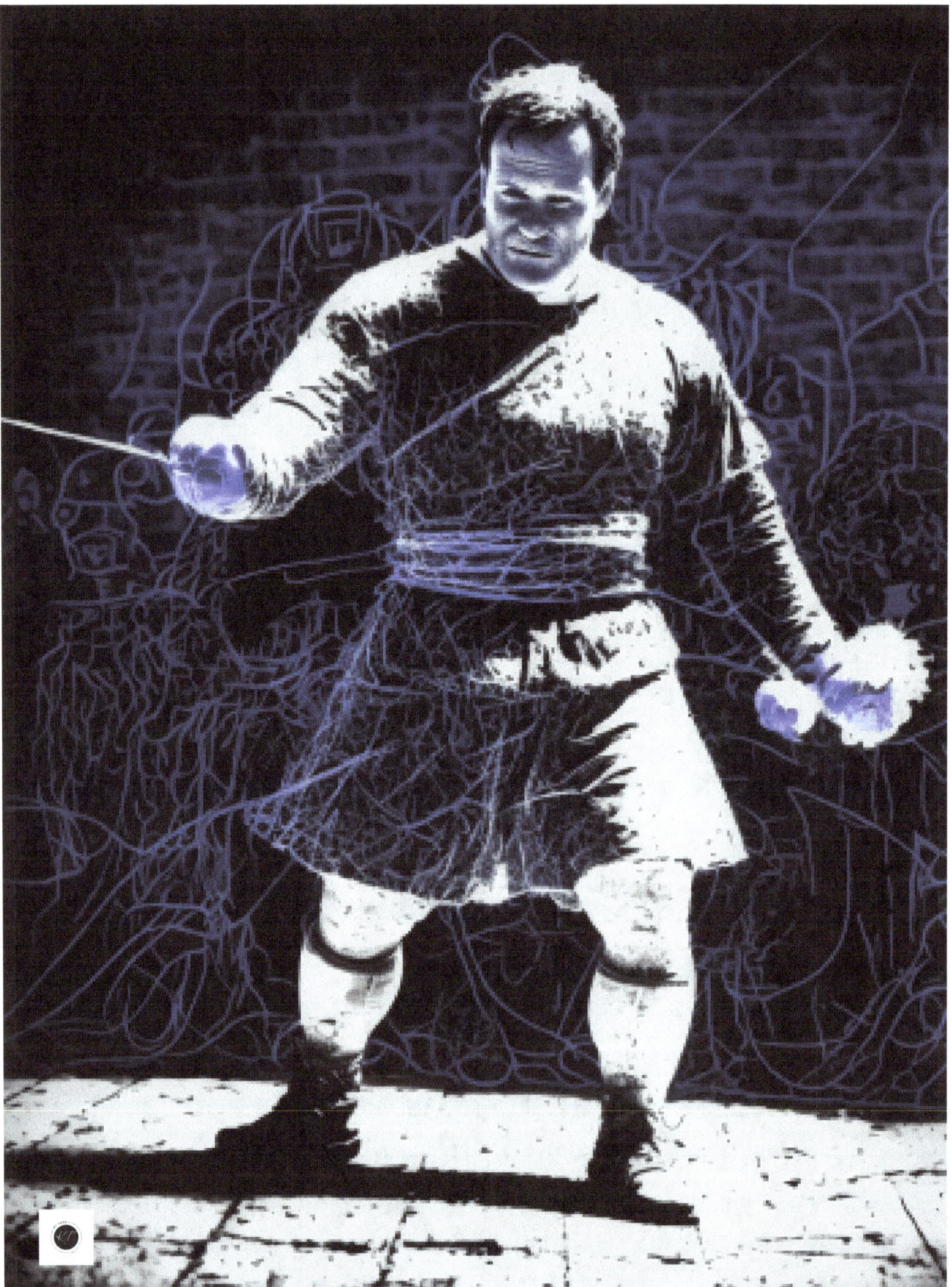

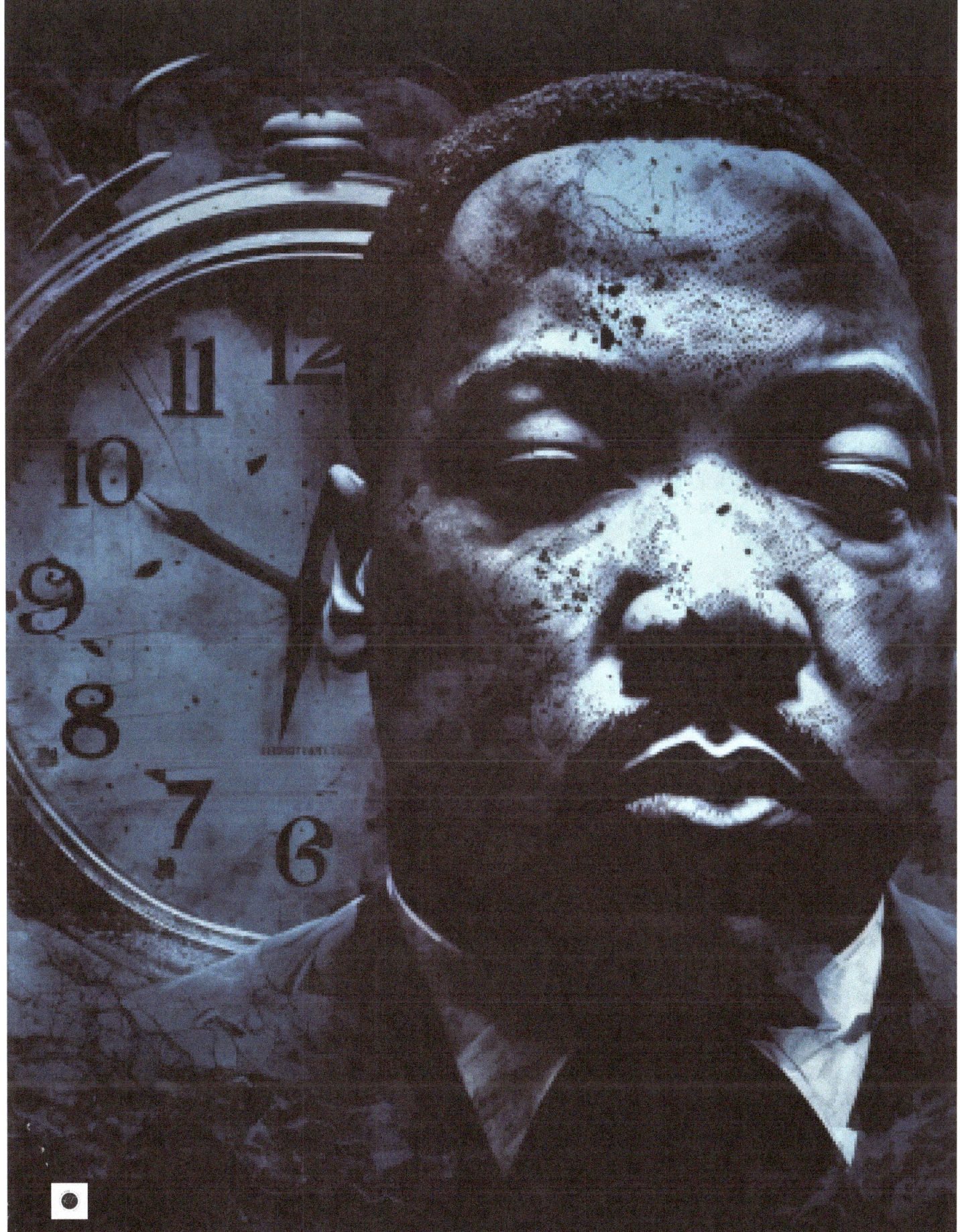

Martin Luther KING JR

If Martin Luther King Jr. were a drum major it would symbolize his innate ability to lead and inspire others. As a drum major, he would be responsible for guiding the tempo, direction, and overall performance of the ensemble, much like how he led the Civil Rights Movement and influenced social change in the United States.

Dr. King often spoke about being a "drum major for justice," which emphasizes his commitment to leading others in the pursuit of equality and fairness. He was all that.

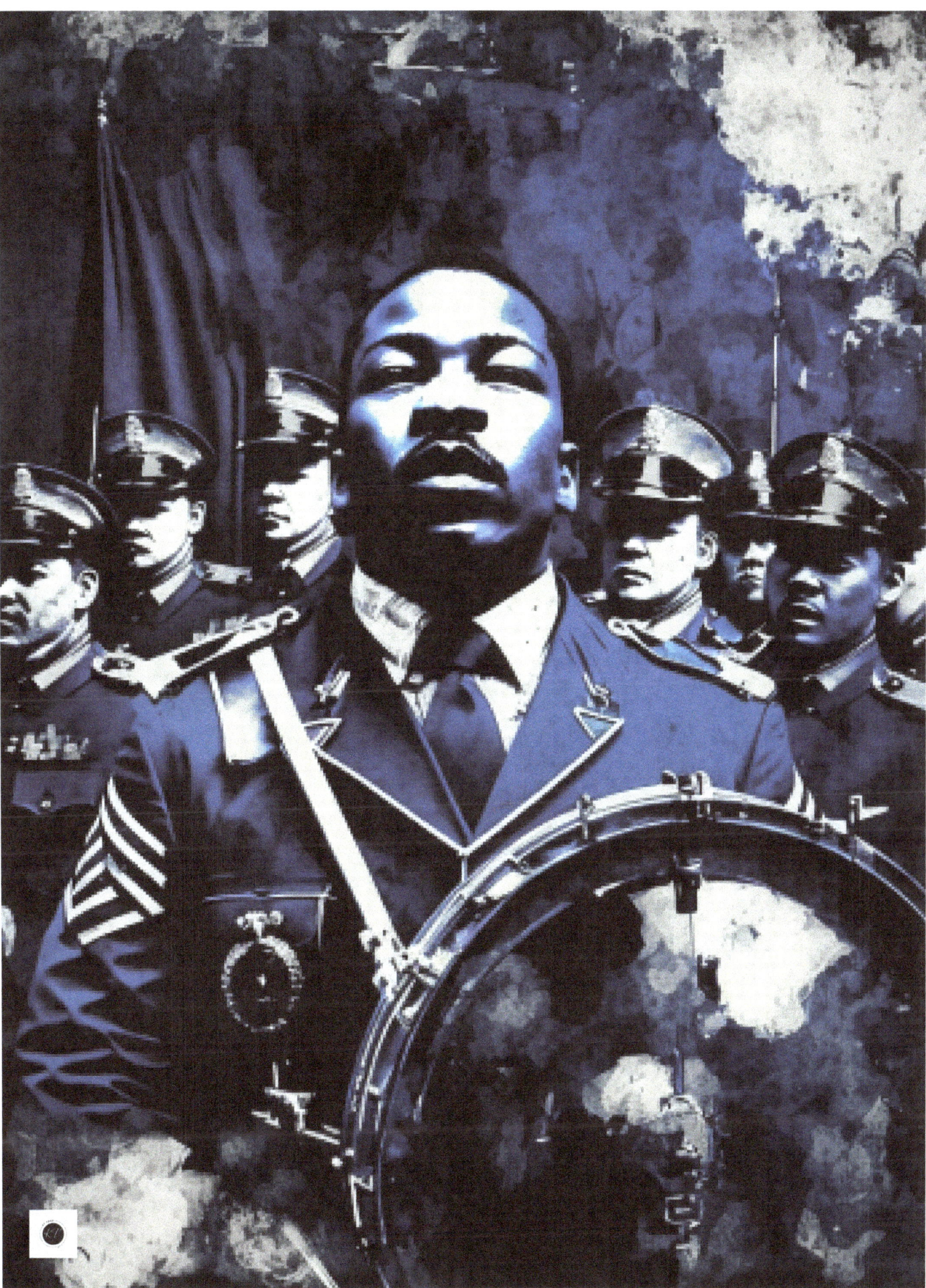

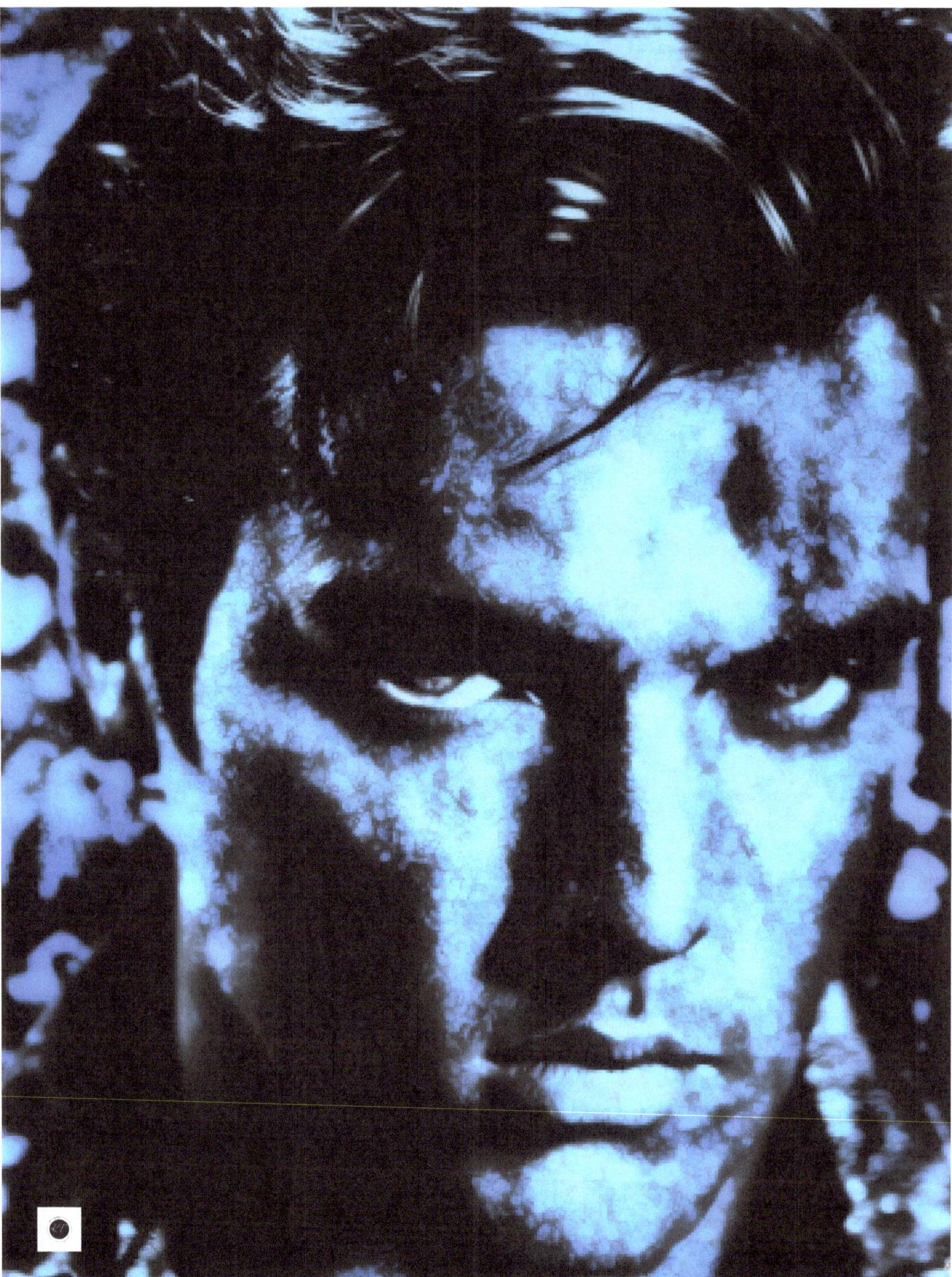

Elvis Pressley

Elvis Presley as a football player combines athleticism, teamwork, and entertainment value, which aligns well with his energetic stage presence and his ability to captivate audiences.

As a charismatic and talented performer, Elvis could be imagined as a quarterback or running back, positions that require agility, speed, and the ability to make show-stopping plays.

These roles would allow Elvis to showcase his flair for the dramatic and his natural talent for engaging with fans, both on and off the field. He would probably sneak over to watch some HBCU games, learn a few things.

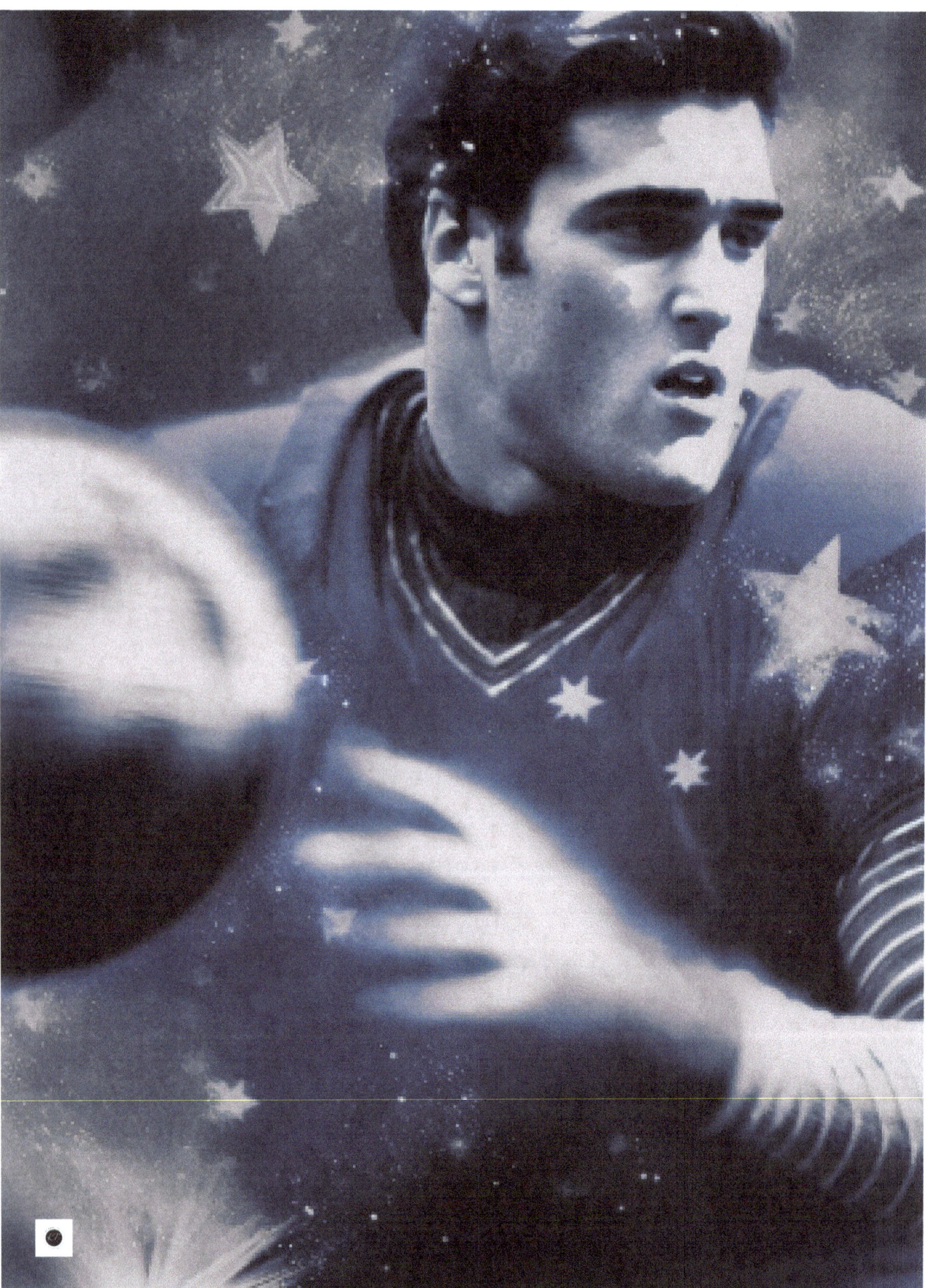

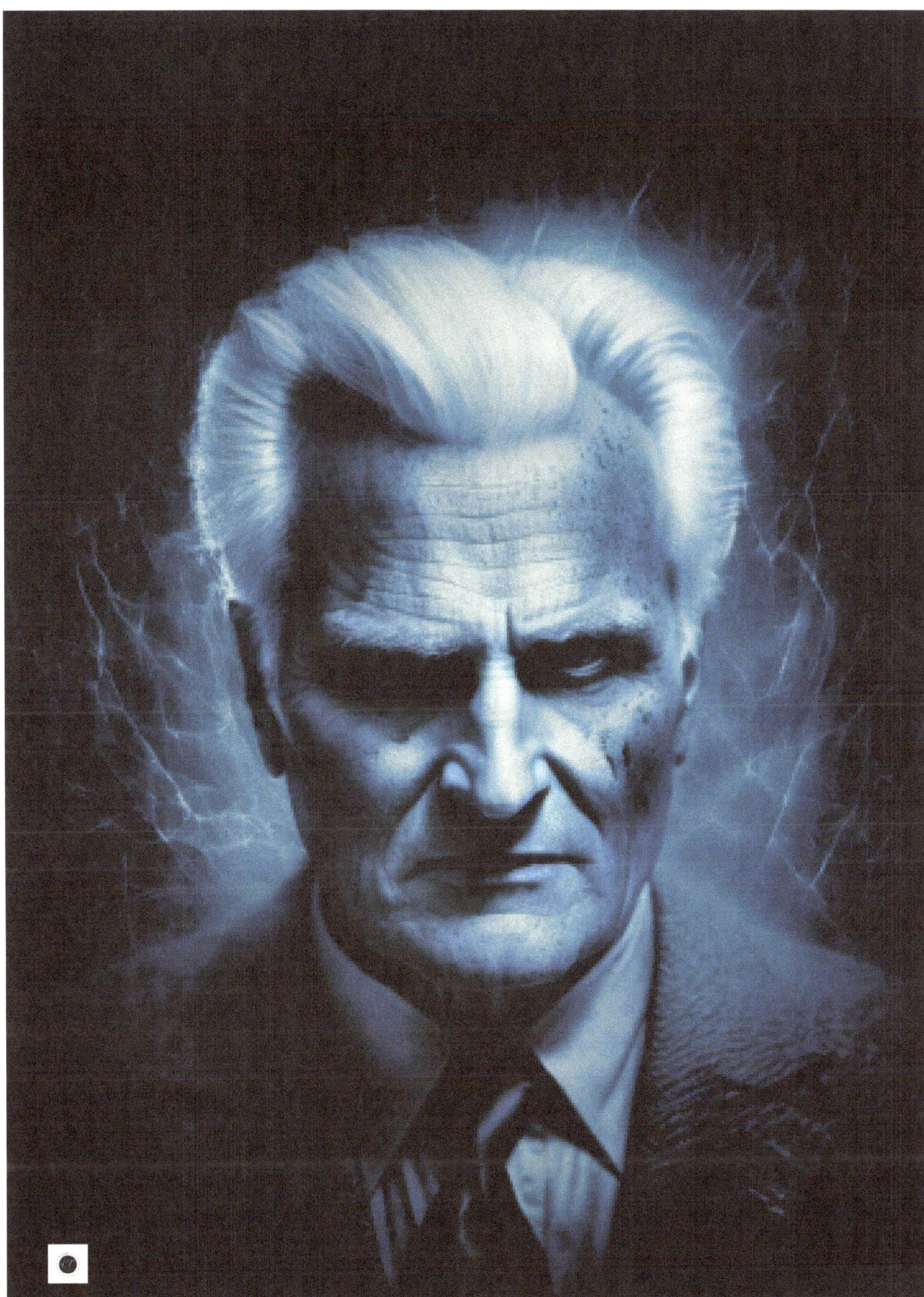

Billy Graham

Billy Graham as a fisherman would emphasize his patience, wisdom, and ability to connect with people on a spiritual level. Fishing is an activity that requires a combination of calmness, persistence, and thought, which align with Graham's talent as a preacher and his ability to captivate audiences through his sermons.

This role would also highlight his capacity for introspection and his deep connection with faith, as fishing can be a meditative and reflective activity. Surely, the big one would never get away!

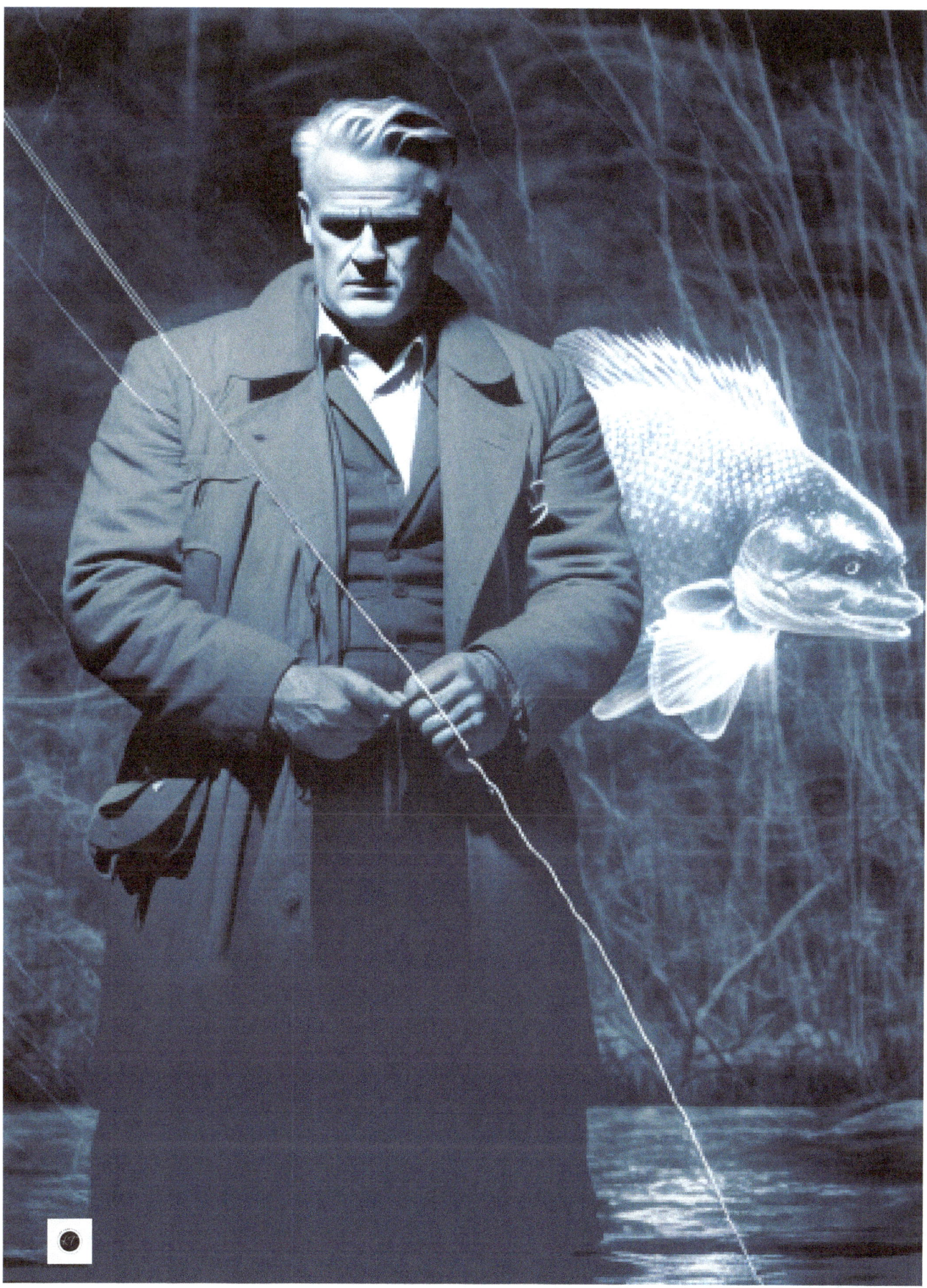

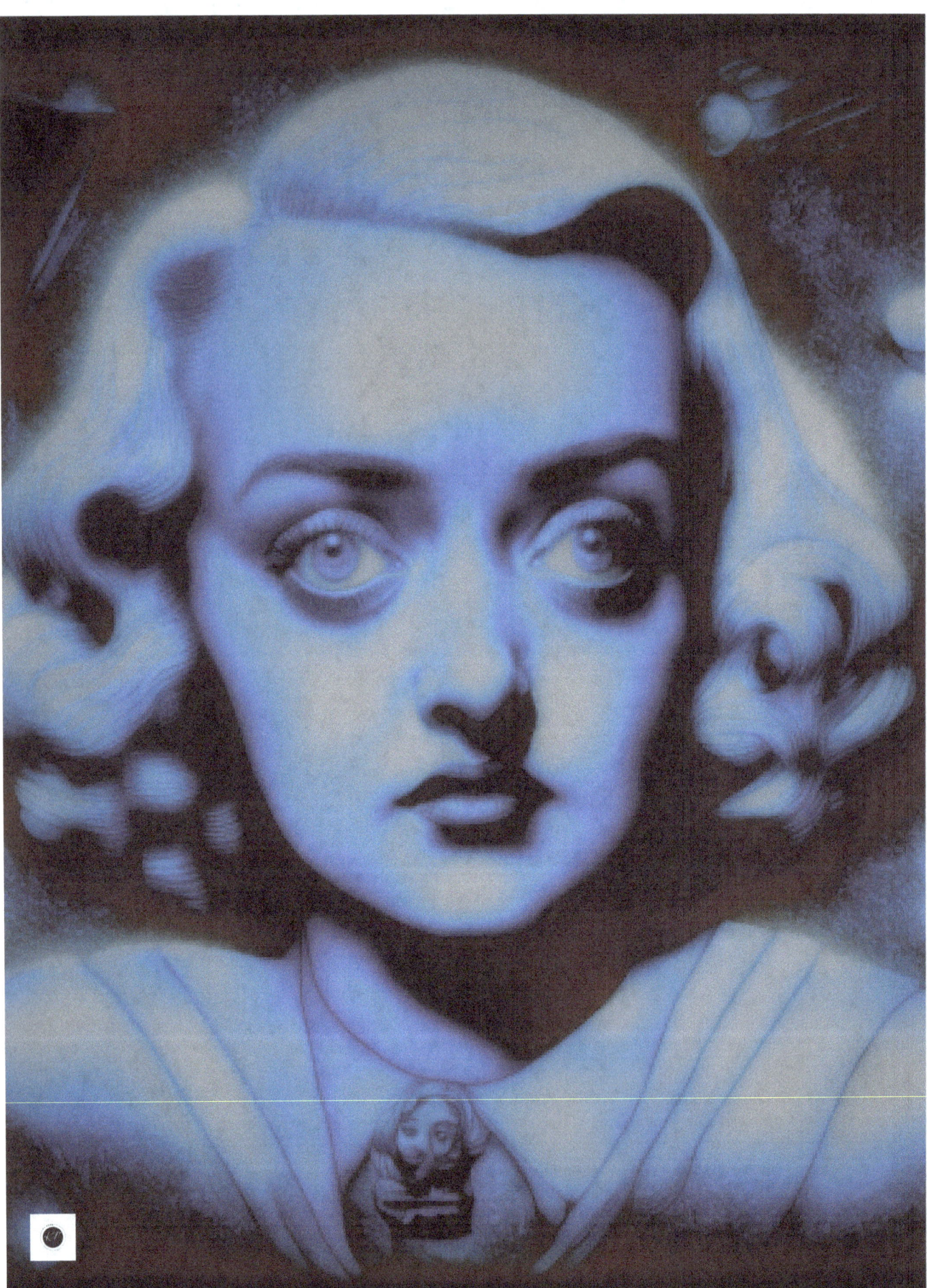

Bette Davis

A fitting sport for her would be tennis. Tennis is a sport that requires a combination of grace, agility, and fierce determination, which aligns well with Bette Davis's strong-willed and sophisticated persona as an actress

Additionally, tennis showcases individual talent and skill while also allowing for moments of drama and intensity, reflecting Davis's captivating on-screen presence. Plus, she'd definitely have the eye's for it.

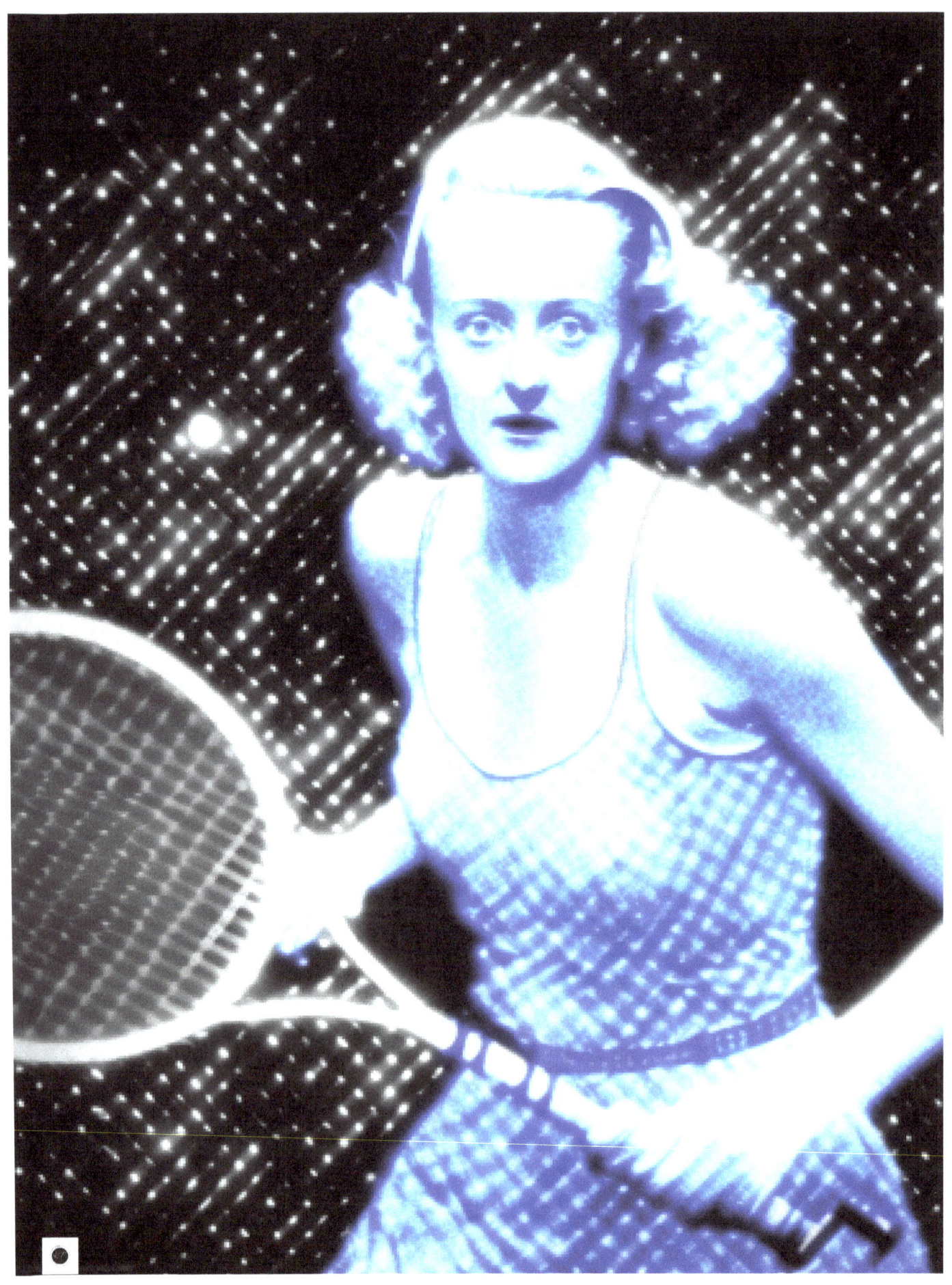

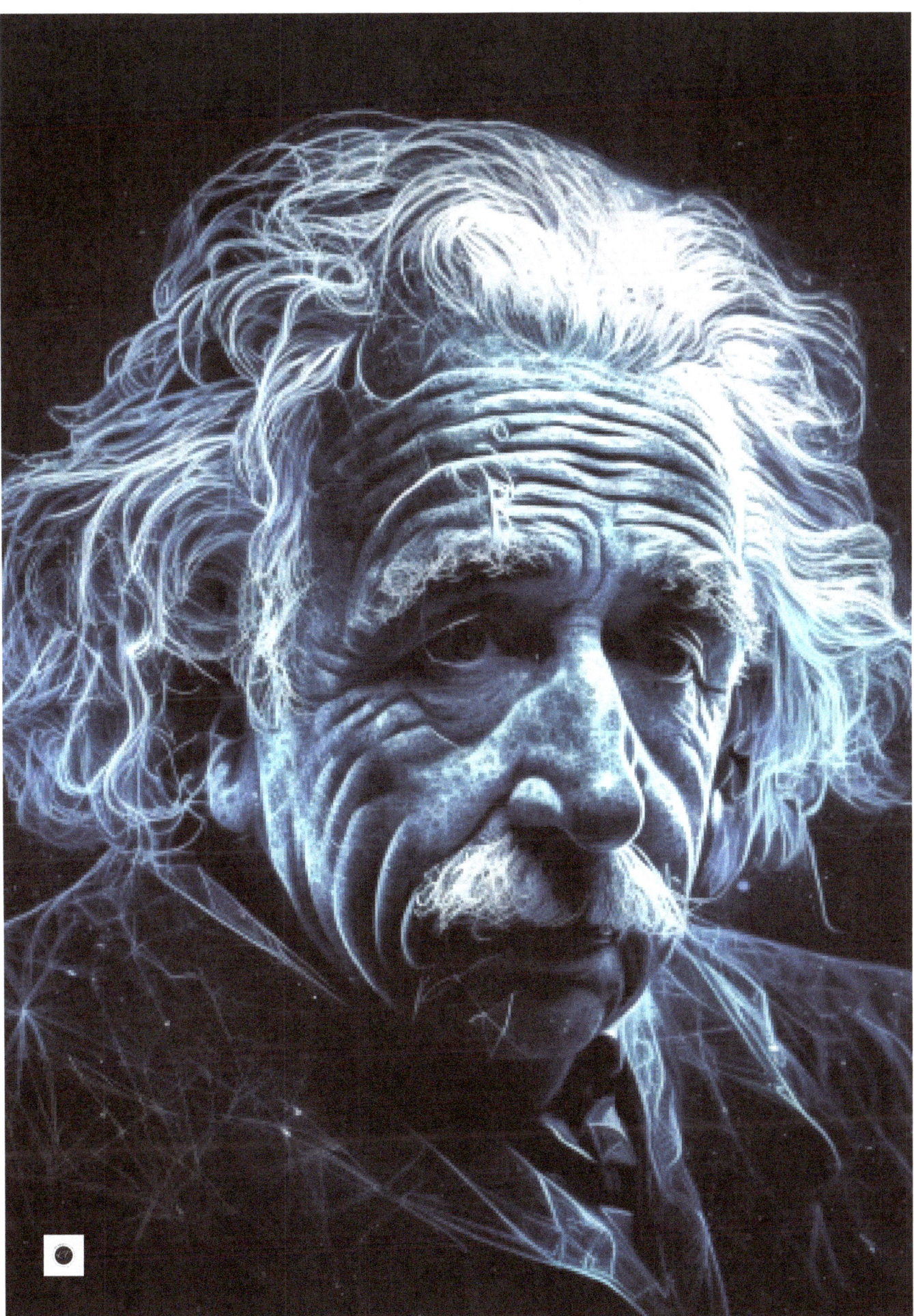

Albert Einstein

Albert Einstein as a chess player would emphasize his incredible intellect, strategic thinking, and ability to analyze complex problems. Chess is a game that requires a combination of logic, foresight, and creativity, which aligns with Einstein's talent as a physicist and his groundbreaking contributions to the world of science.

As a chess player, Einstein would showcase his mental acuity, focus, and adaptability, much like how he revolutionized scientific thought through his development of the theory of relativity and other groundbreaking ideas.

This role would also highlight his capacity for deep concentration and his fascination with understanding the underlying principles that govern the universe. And, all that brain power made Albert...amorous.

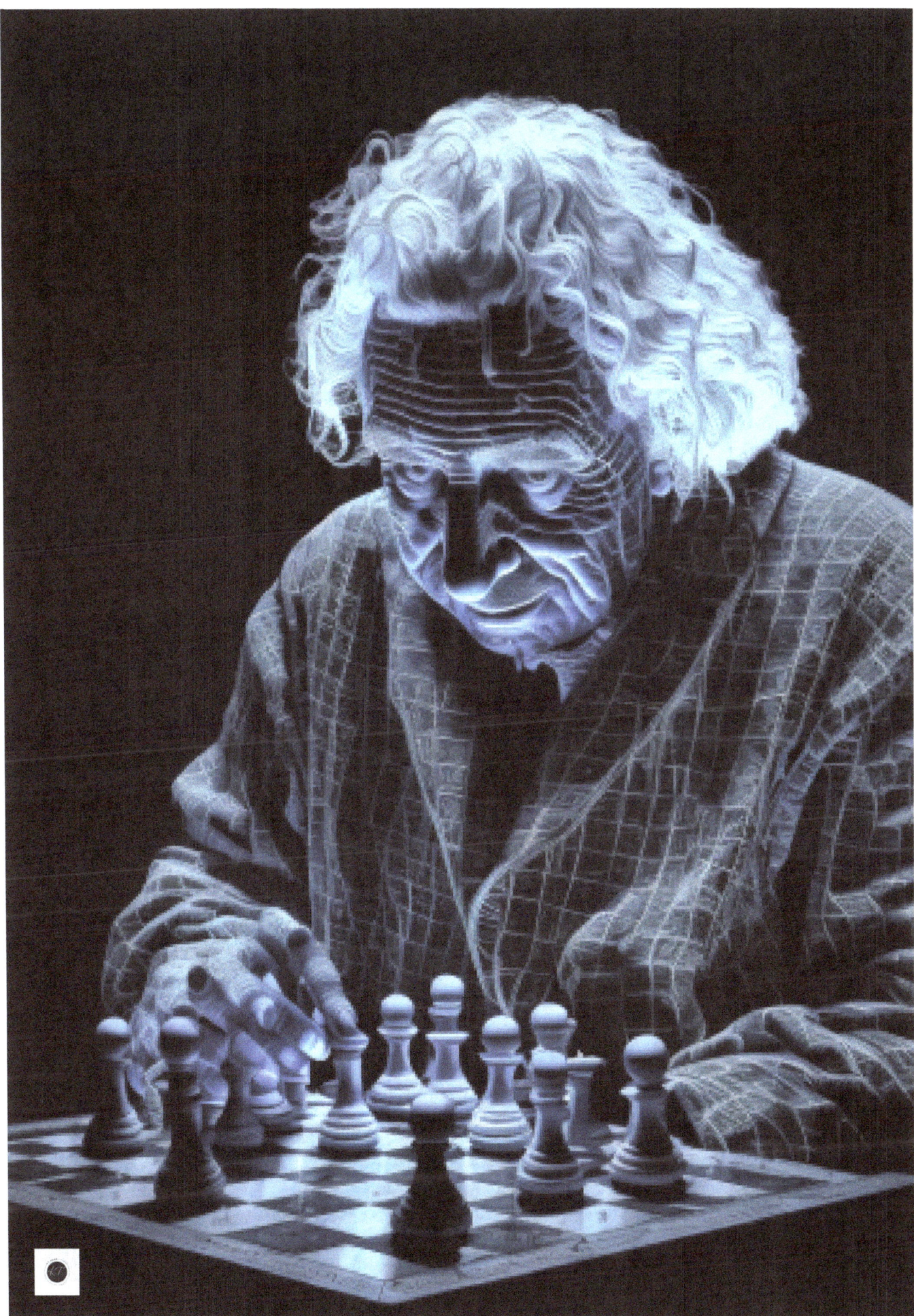

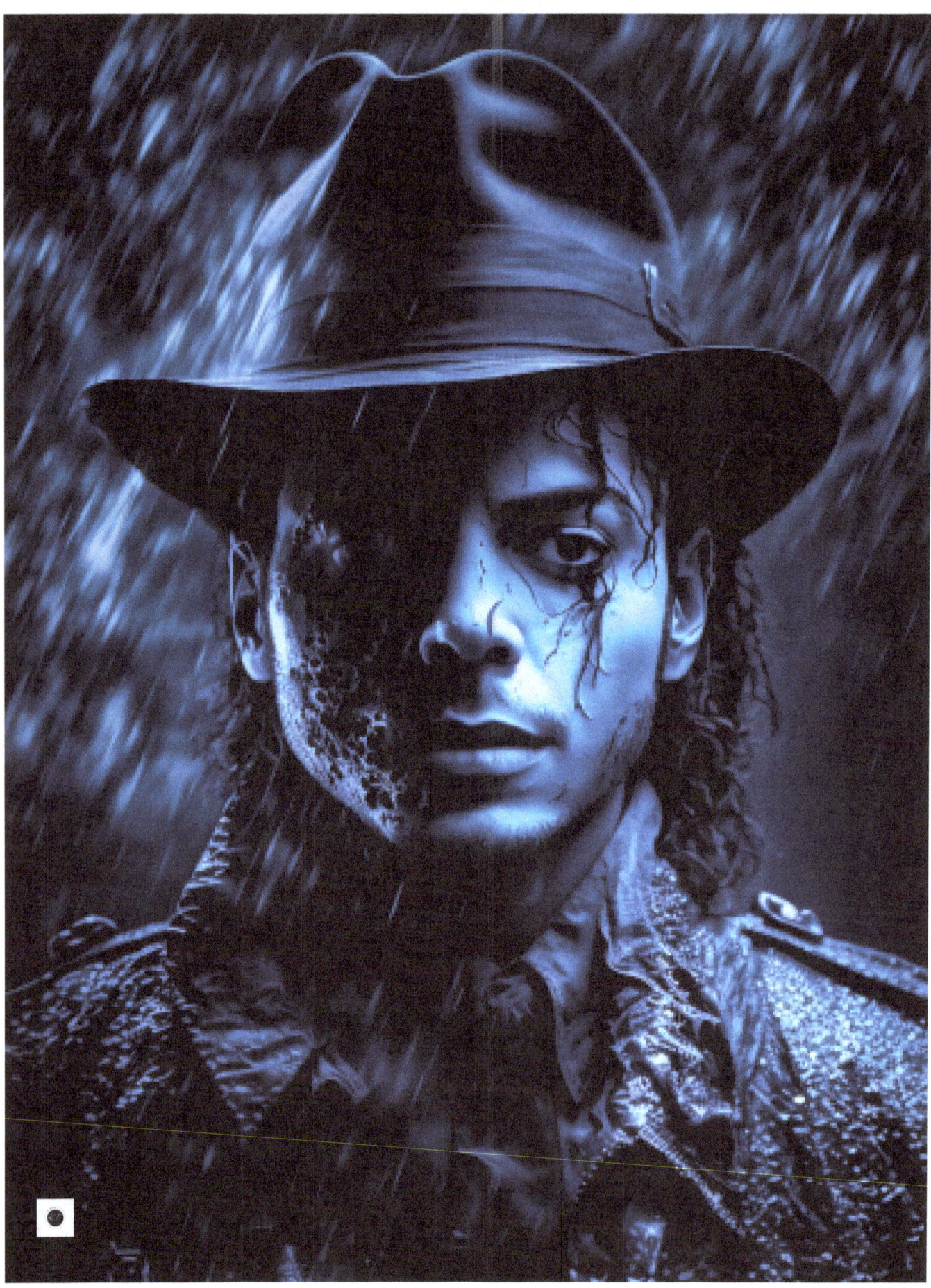

Michael Jackson

Michael Jackson as a ping pong player would emphasize his agility, quick reflexes, and ability to entertain audiences through his incredible performances. Ping pong, or table tennis, is a sport that requires a combination of speed, coordination, and precision, which aligns with Jackson's talent as a singer, dancer, and performer.

As a ping pong player, Michael Jackson would showcase his swift reflexes, focus, and adaptability, much like how he captivated audiences around the world with his groundbreaking music and mesmerizing dance moves. This role highlights his capacity for concentration and his ability to excel, as ping pong matches can be fast-paced and intense. But, he should never play Prince, he did once. Lost.

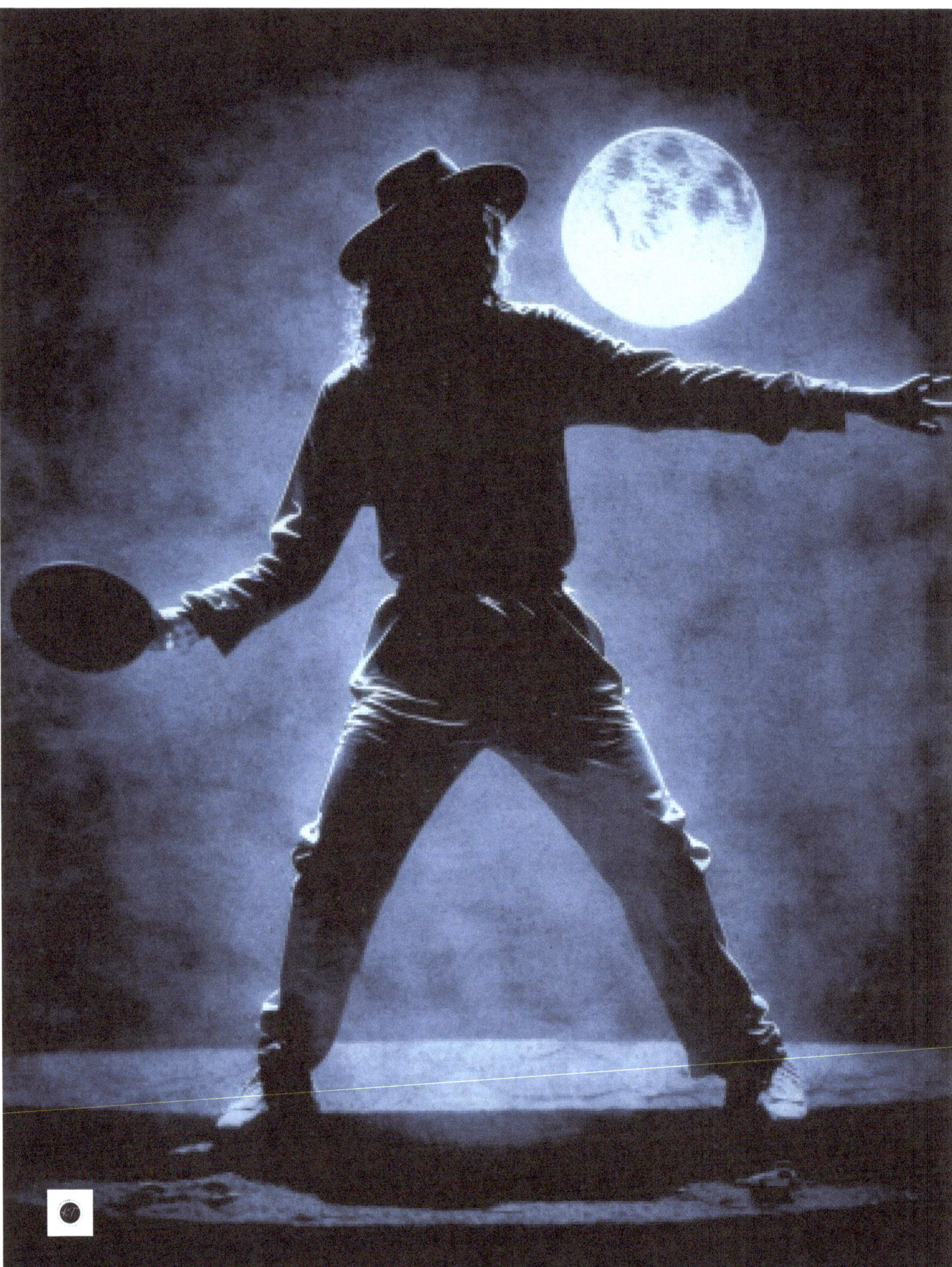

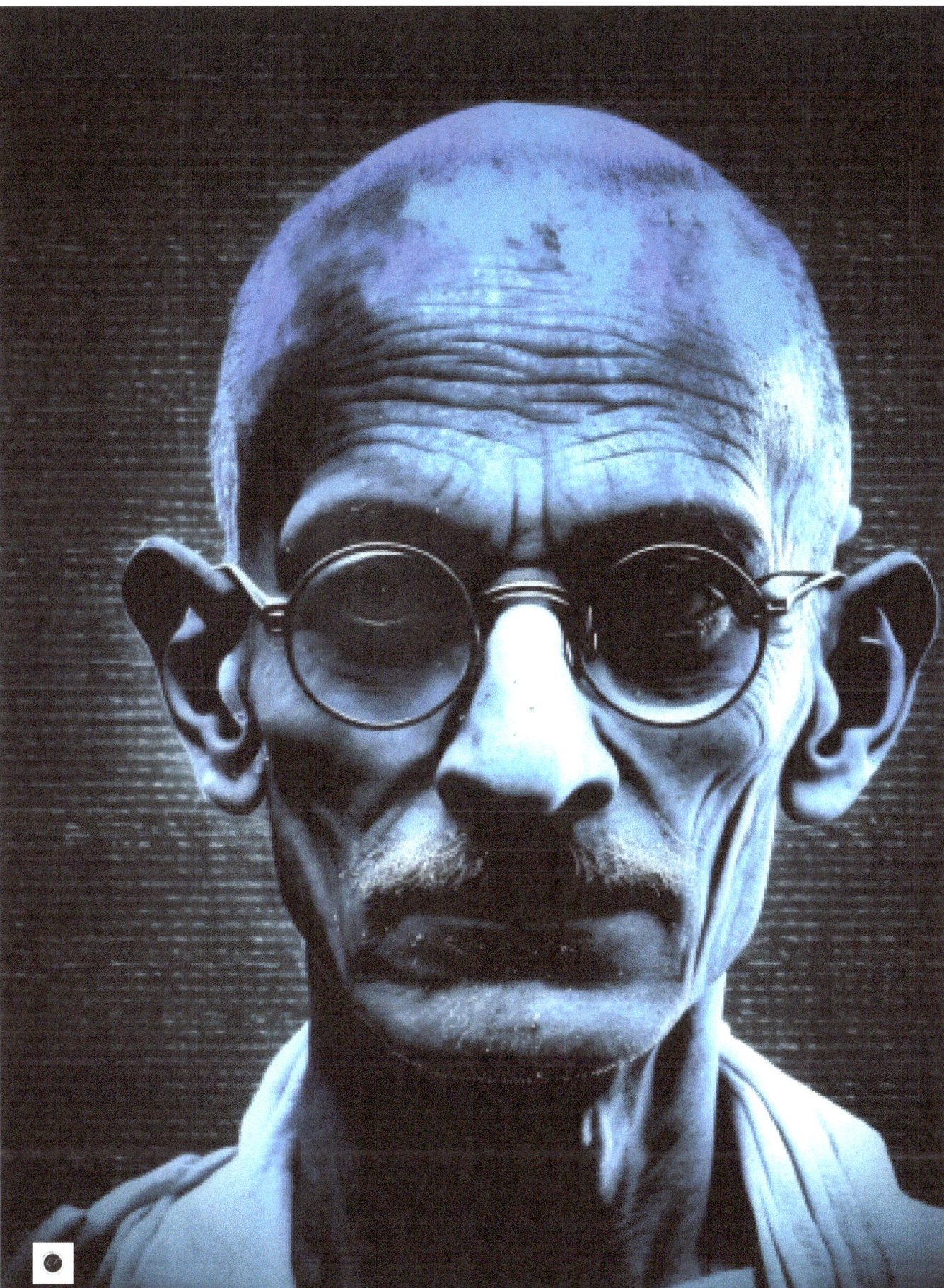

Mahatma Ghandi

As a yoga instructor, Mahatma Gandhi would showcase his serenity, focus, and adaptability, much like how he captivated the hearts of people around the world with his principles of nonviolent protest and his unwavering commitment to justice and equality.

This role would also highlight his capacity for introspection, his ability to guide others on their spiritual journeys, and his resilience, as yoga practice can be challenging and requires both physical and mental strength. Hopefully, he'd see African's in a different light.

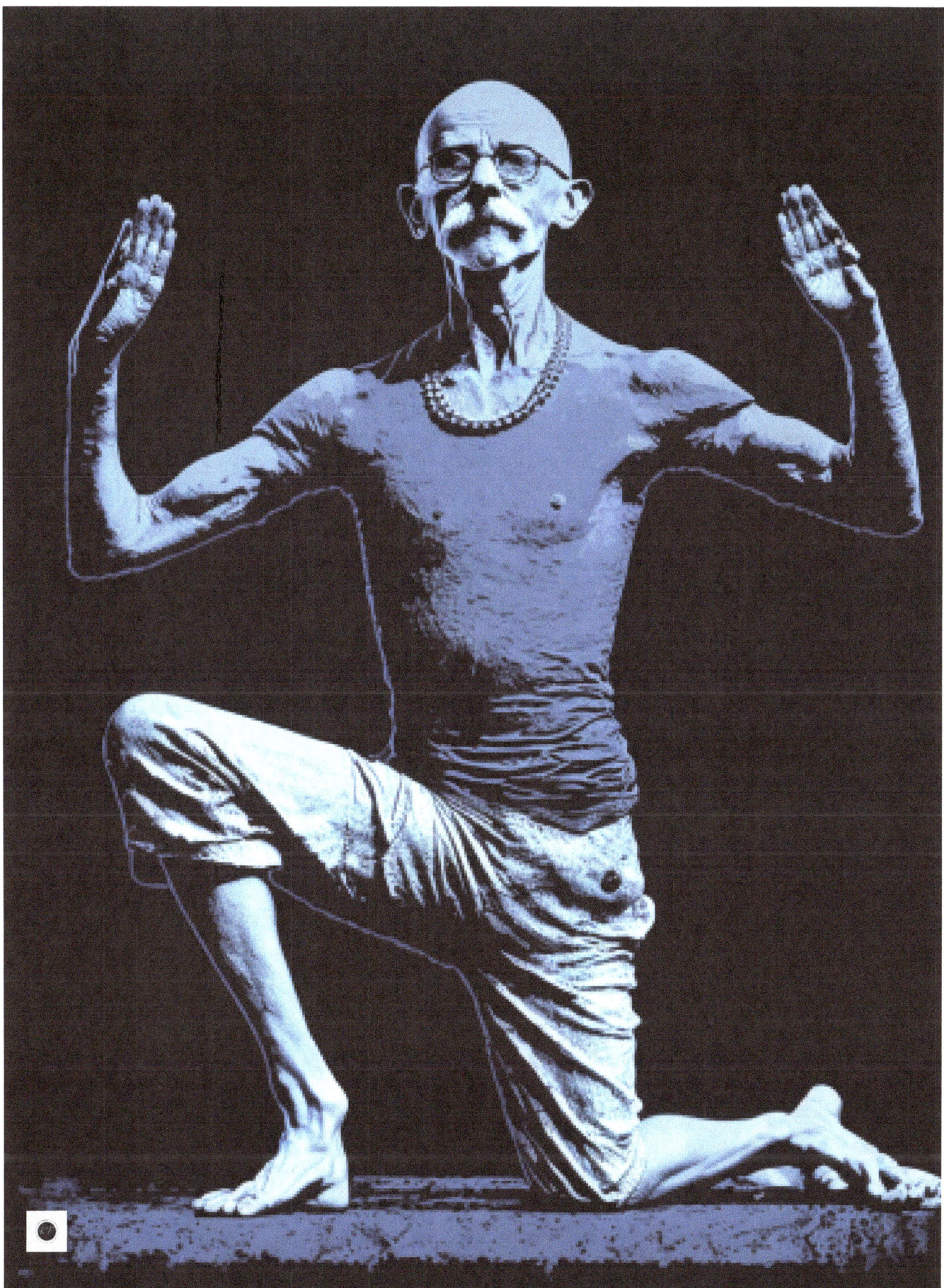

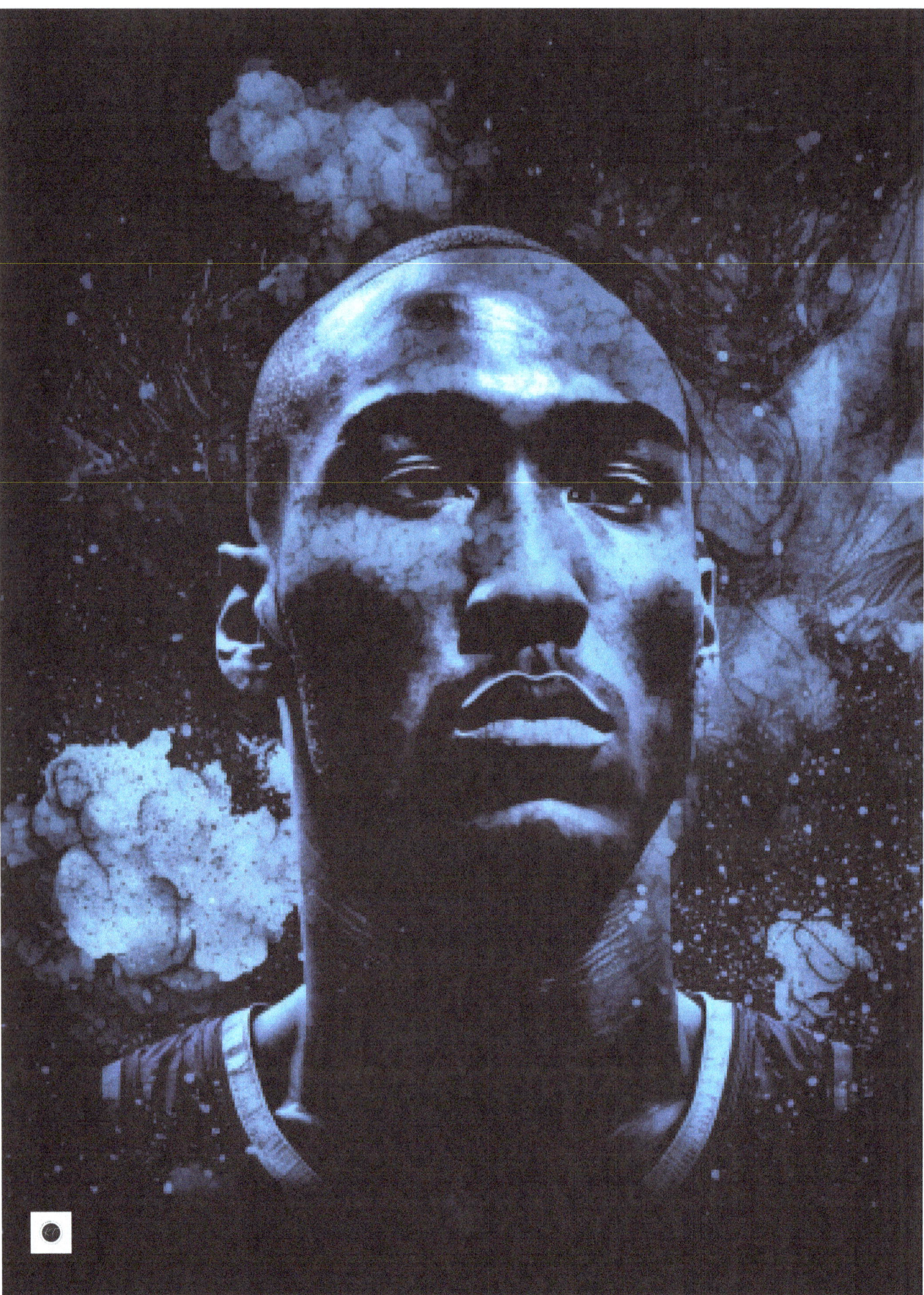

Kobe Bryant

Kobe Bryant as a saxophone player would emphasize his dedication, discipline, and ability to captivate audiences with his exceptional talent. Playing the saxophone is an art form that requires a combination of technical skill, creativity, and emotional expression, which aligns with Bryant's talent as a basketball player .

As a sax player, Kobe Bryant would showcase his determination, focus, much like how he mesmerized fans with his incredible basketball skills and his work ethic. This role would also highlight his capacity for concentration, his ability to perform under pressure, and his drive for excellence, as mastering a musical instrument demands a high level of commitment and practice. One thing though, just keep Shaq out of the band.

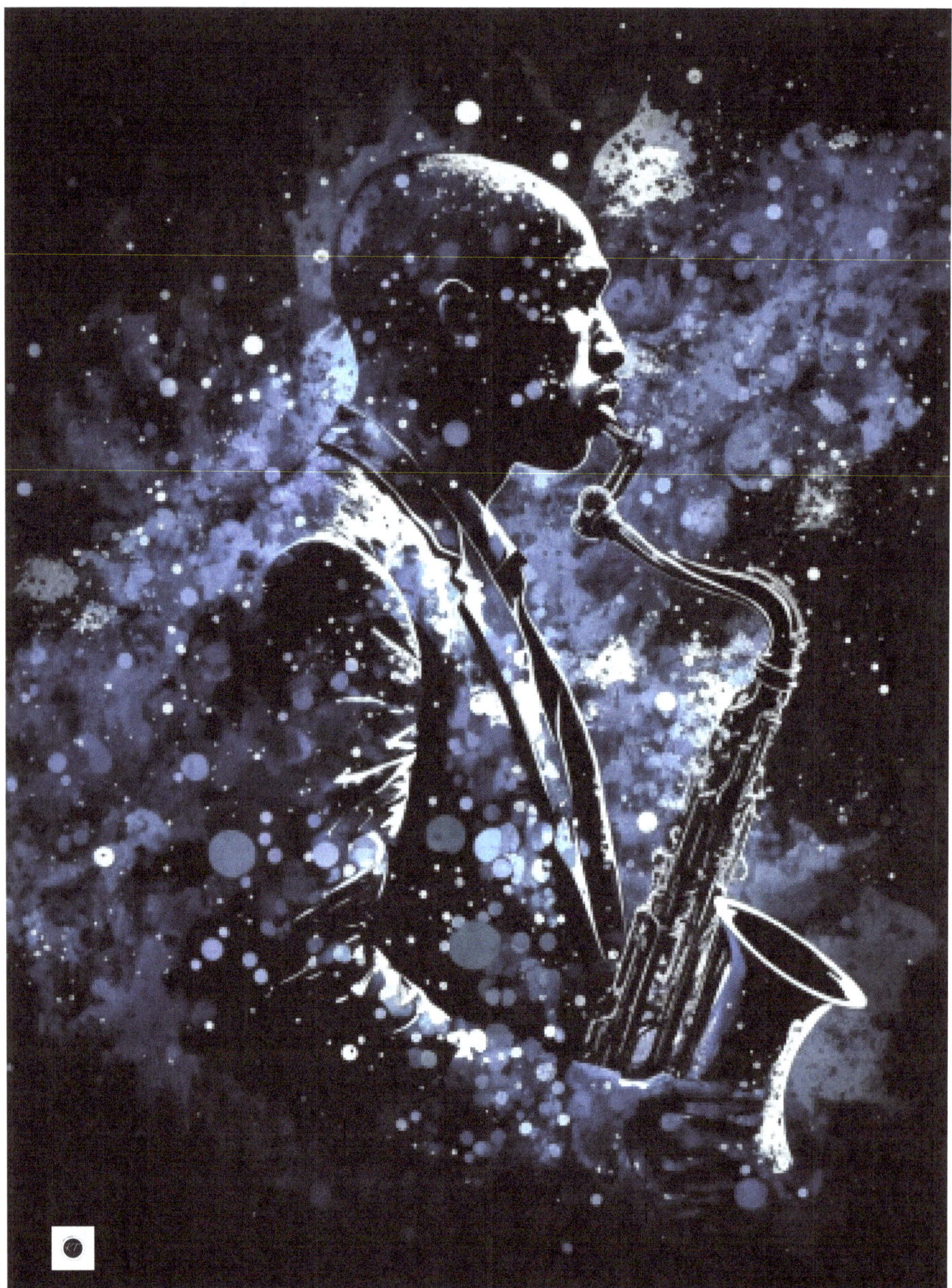

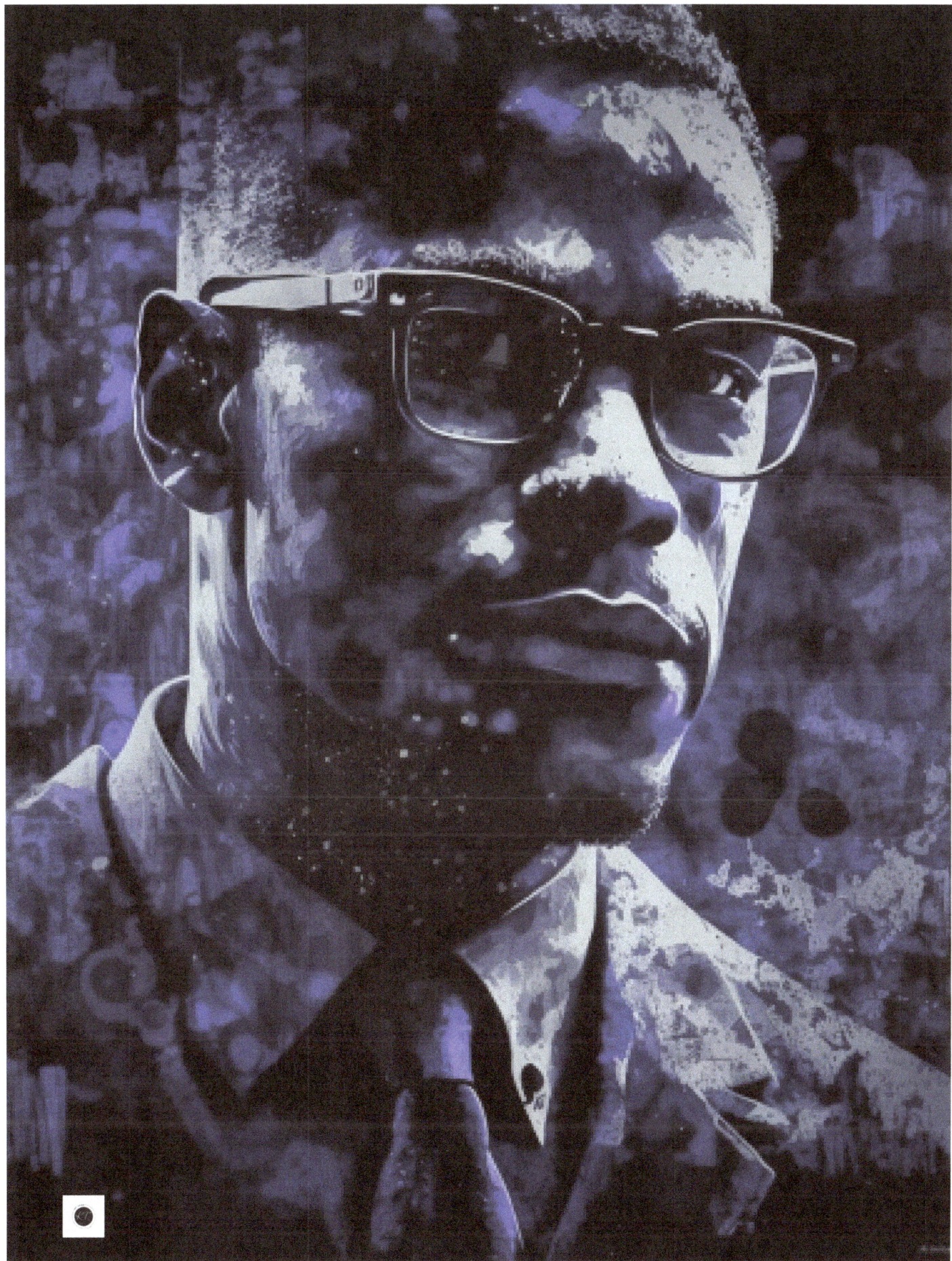

Malcolm X

Malcolm X were to be portrayed as an athlete, he would fit well as a boxer. Boxing is a sport that requires physical strength, mental fortitude, and strategic thinking, qualities that align with Malcolm X's strong character and his role as a civil rights leader.

Just like a boxer, Malcolm X fought for his beliefs and advocated for the rights and self-defense of African Americans during a time of widespread racial injustice. Oh, what he'd say today.

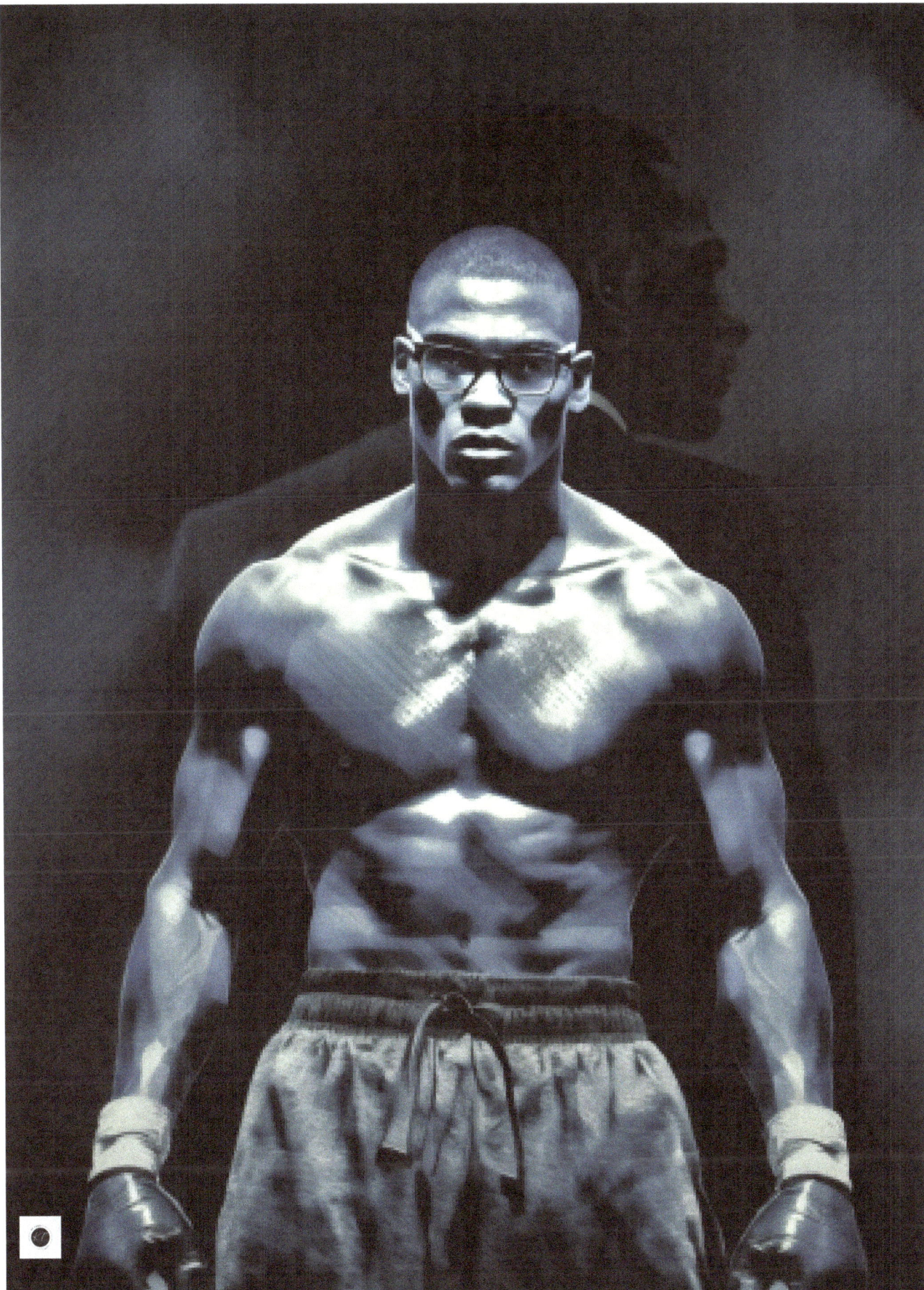

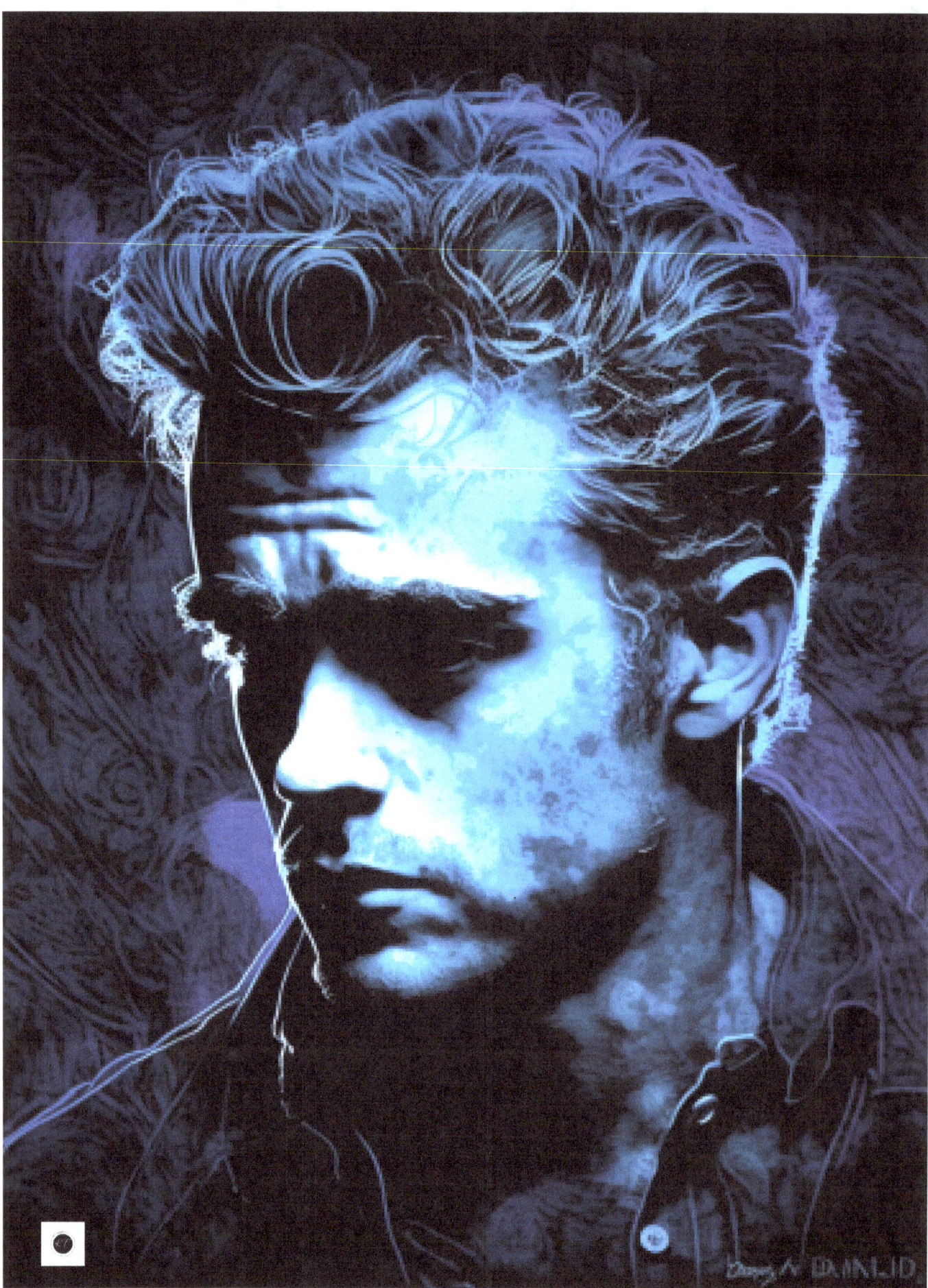

James Dean

James Dean as a motocross racer would emphasize his passion for adventure, bold spirit, and ability to captivate audiences with his magnetic presence. Motocross racing requires skill, fearlessness, and physical prowess, which aligns with Dean's talent as an actor.

As a motocross racer, James Dean would showcase his determination, focus, and adaptability, much like how he mesmerized fans around the world with his unforgettable performances and his embodiment of the "rebel" persona. This role would also highlight his capacity for taking risks, and his drive for pushing boundaries, as motocross racing demands a high level of commitment, courage, and physical fitness.

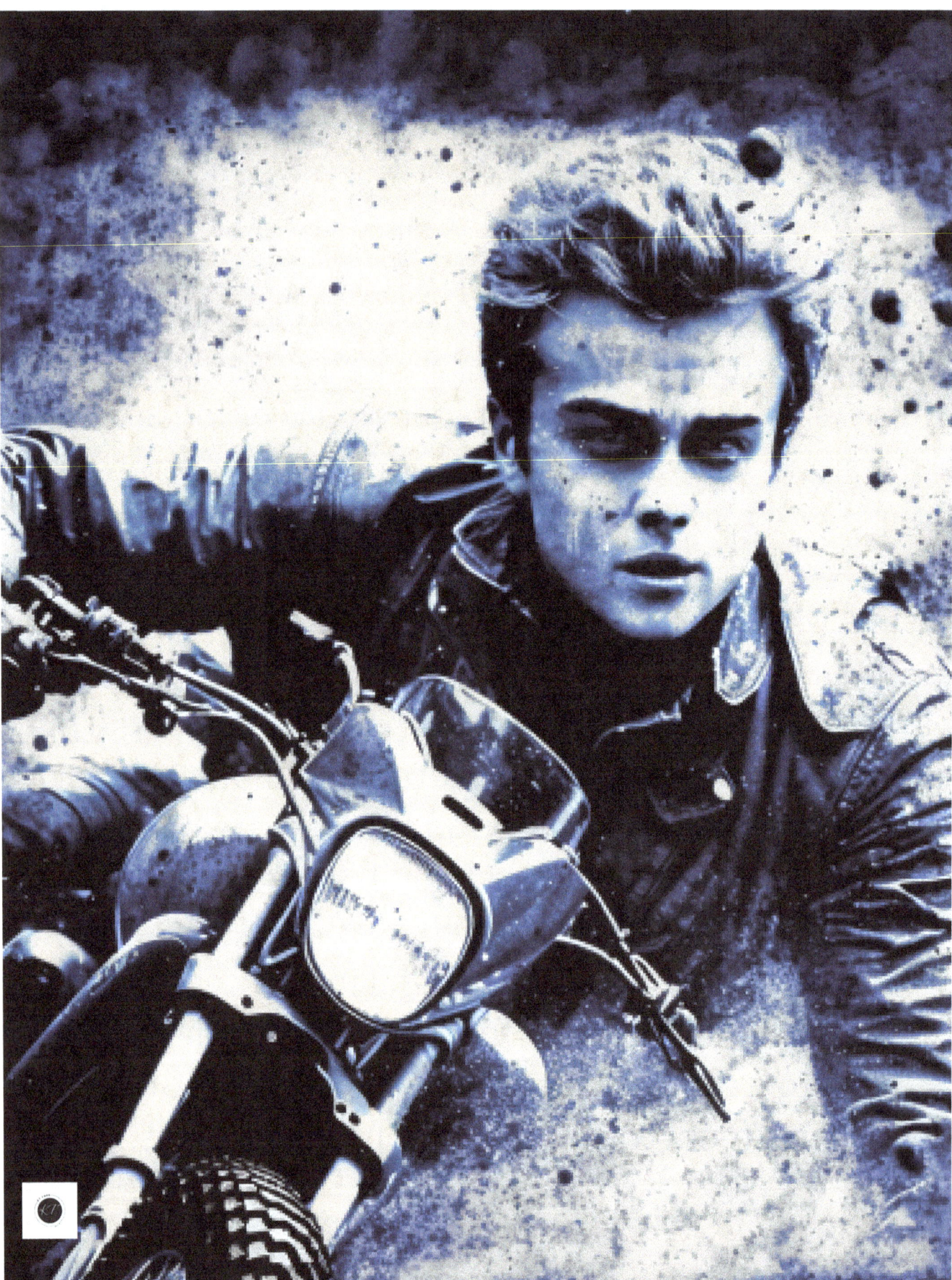

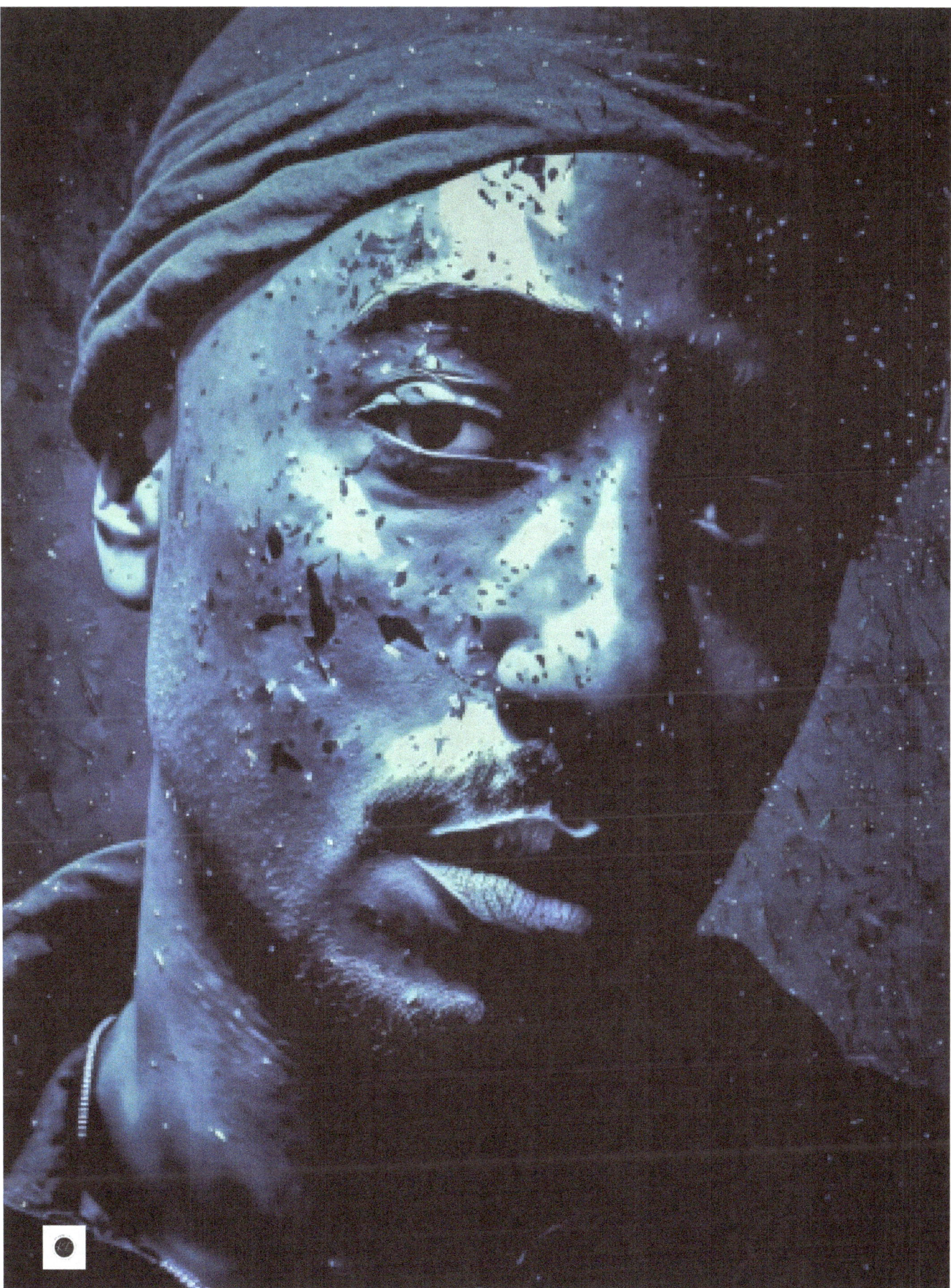

Tupac Shakur

Tupac Shakur as a basketball player would use skill, teamwork, and creativity, which aligns with his talent as a rapper, poet, and actor. As a sport that is deeply connected to urban culture and the African American community, basketball also reflects the themes and issues that Tupac often addressed in his music and activism.

Playing as a point guard or shooting guard, Tupac would be responsible for orchestrating plays and making clutch shots, much like how he captivated audiences with his powerful lyrics and performances. These positions would allow him to showcase his ability to think quickly and adapt to changing circumstances on the court. Plus, he'd teach Dame Lilliard how to really rap!

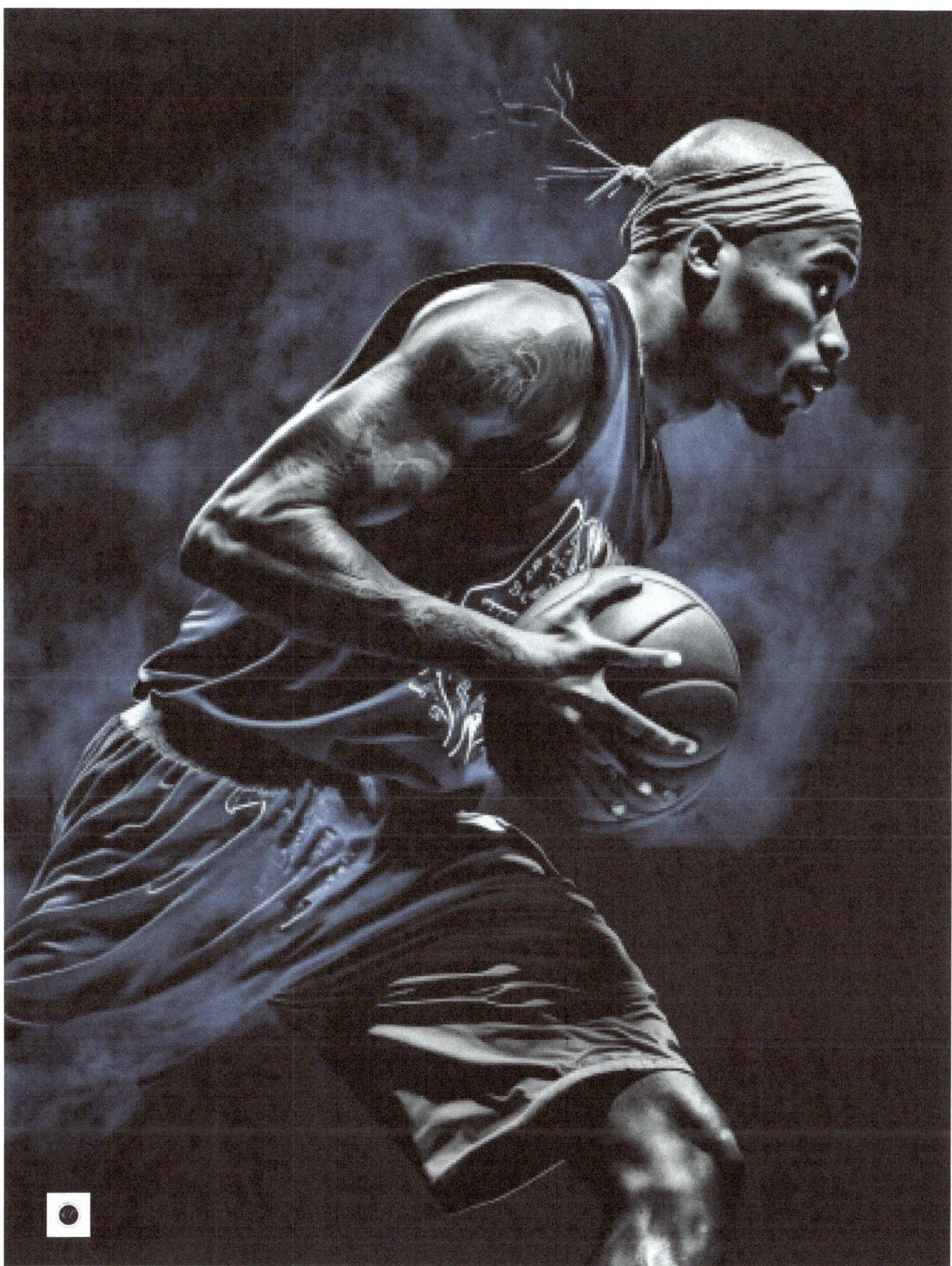

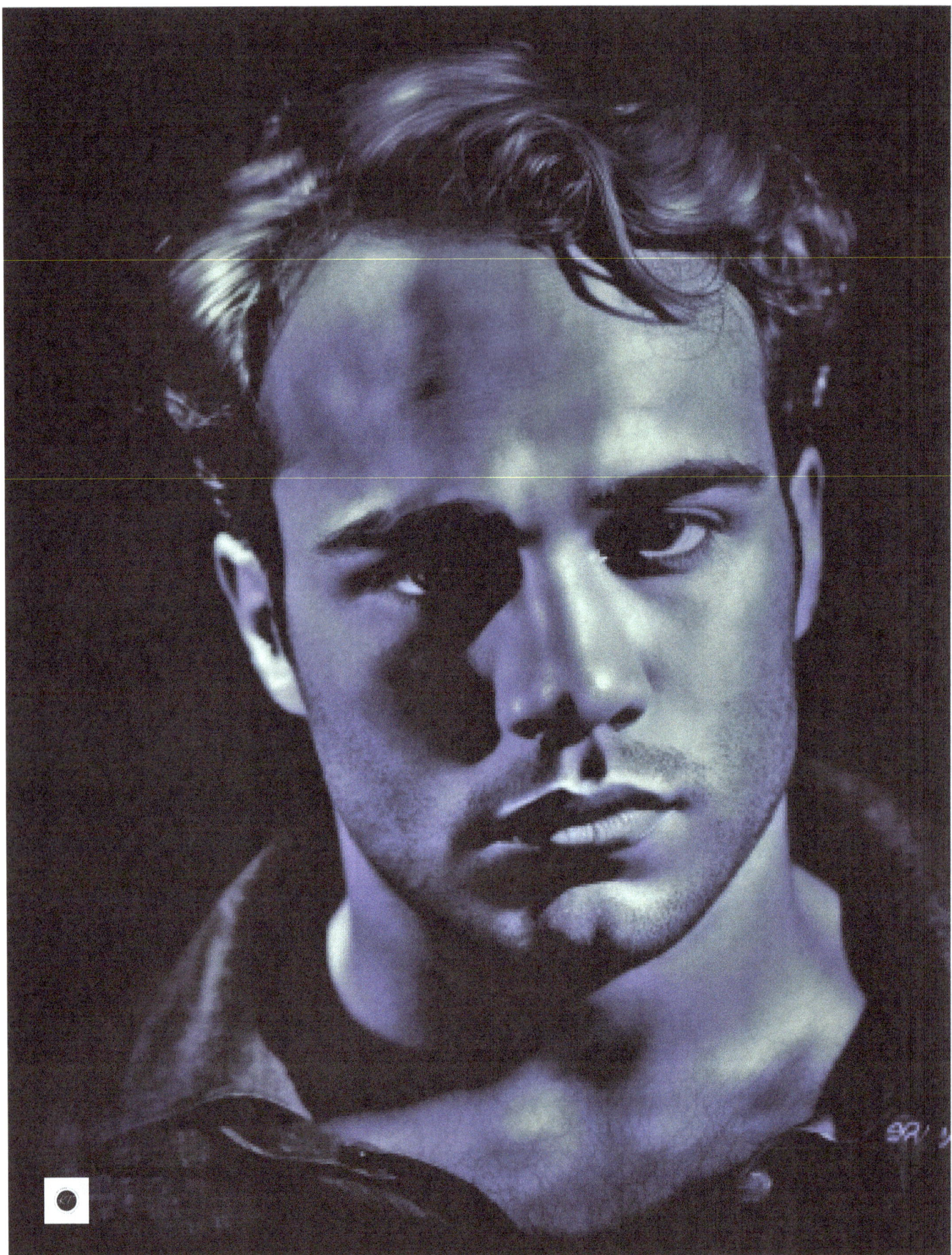

Marlon Brando

Marlon Brando as a ballroom dancer would emphasize his elegance, charisma, and ability to captivate audiences through his powerful presence. Ballroom dancing is an art form that requires a combination of grace, poise, and artistic expression, which align with Brando's talent as an actor and his emotionally nuanced performances.

As a ballroom dancer, Brando would showcase his fluidity, focus, and adaptability, much like how he immersed himself in his acting roles through his method acting approach. This role would also highlight his capacity for deep concentration, dedication to his craft, and the charm and charisma he brought to the screen. Just keep him away from sticks of butter.

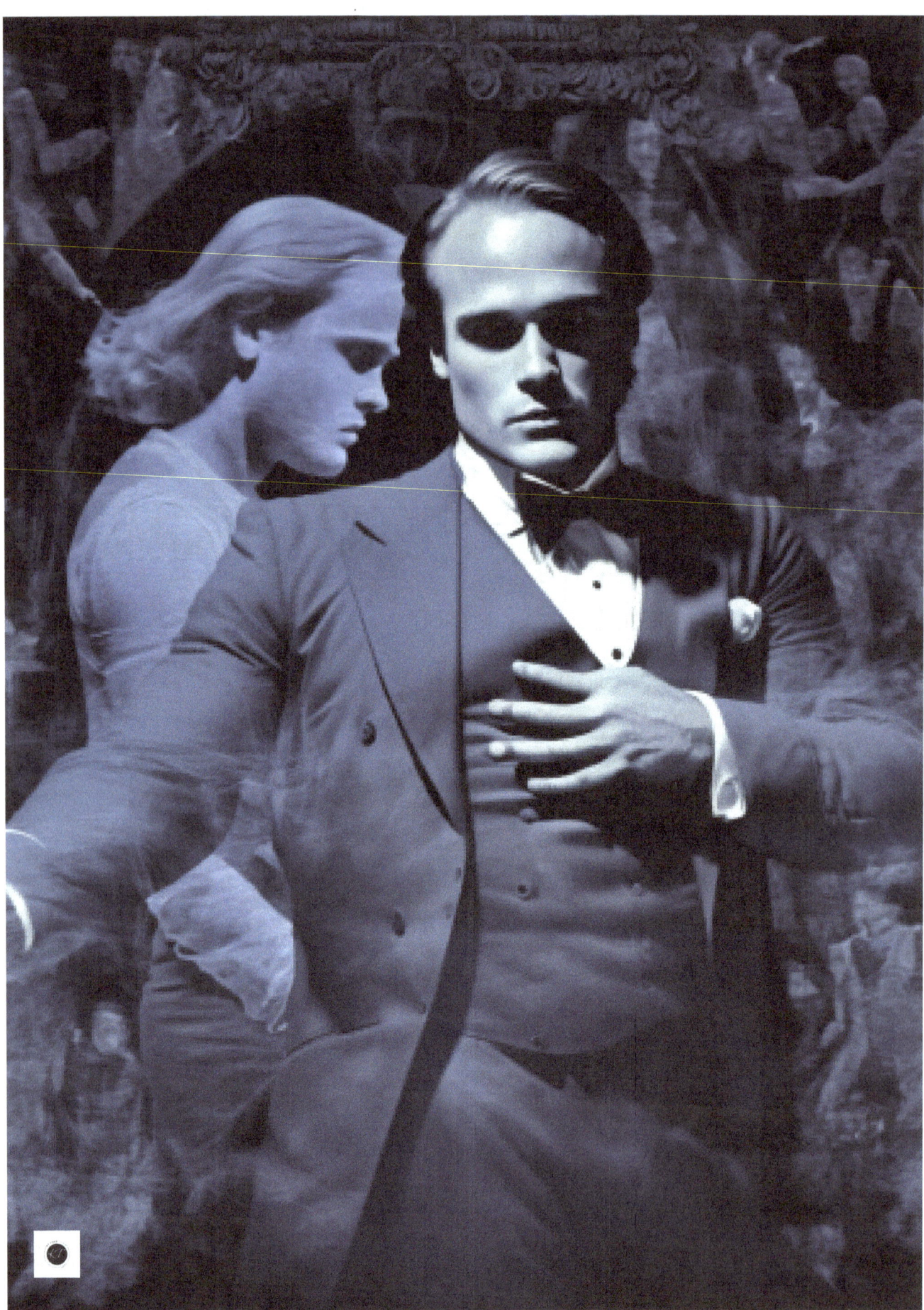

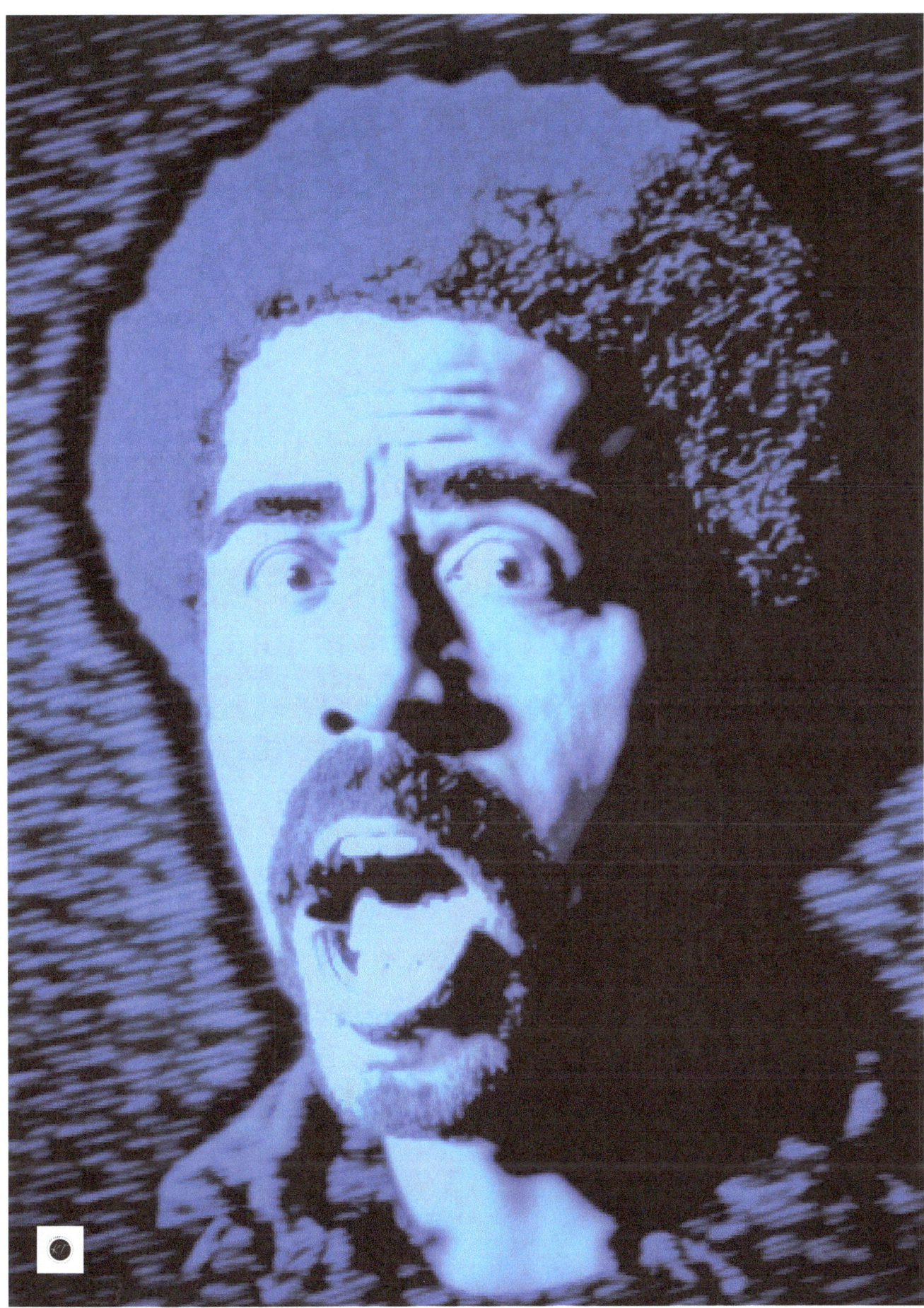

Richard Pryor

Richard Pryor as a bowler would emphasize his precision, focus, and ability to perform under pressure. Bowling is a sport that requires a combination of skill, concentration, and adaptability, which align with Pryor's talent as a comedian and his ability to captivate audiences through his humor and storytelling.

As a bowler, Pryor would showcase his determination, attention to detail, and capacity for deep concentration, much like how he broke barriers with his groundbreaking comedy and daring performances. Now if he invites you to his house for cookies and milk, decline!

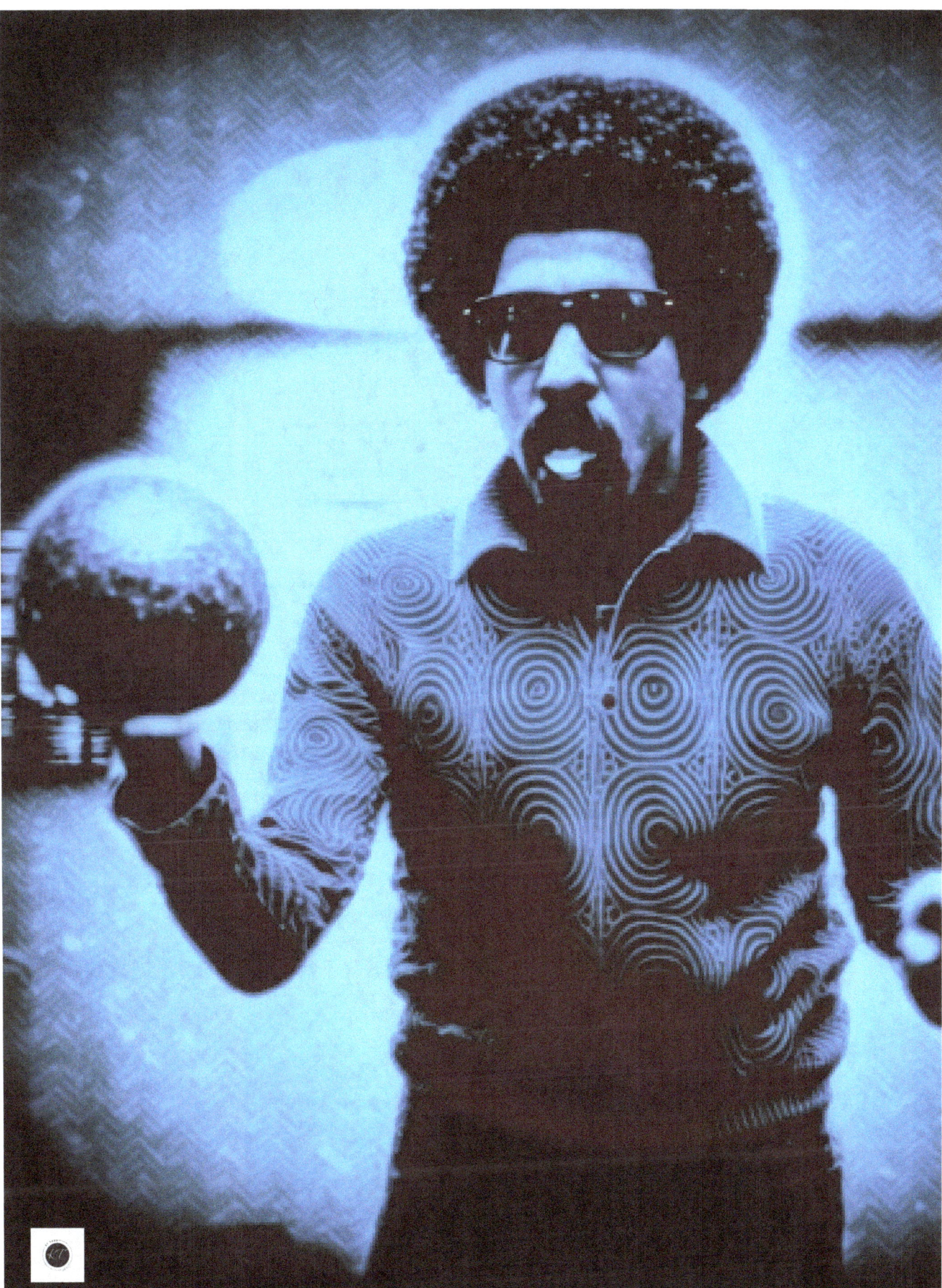

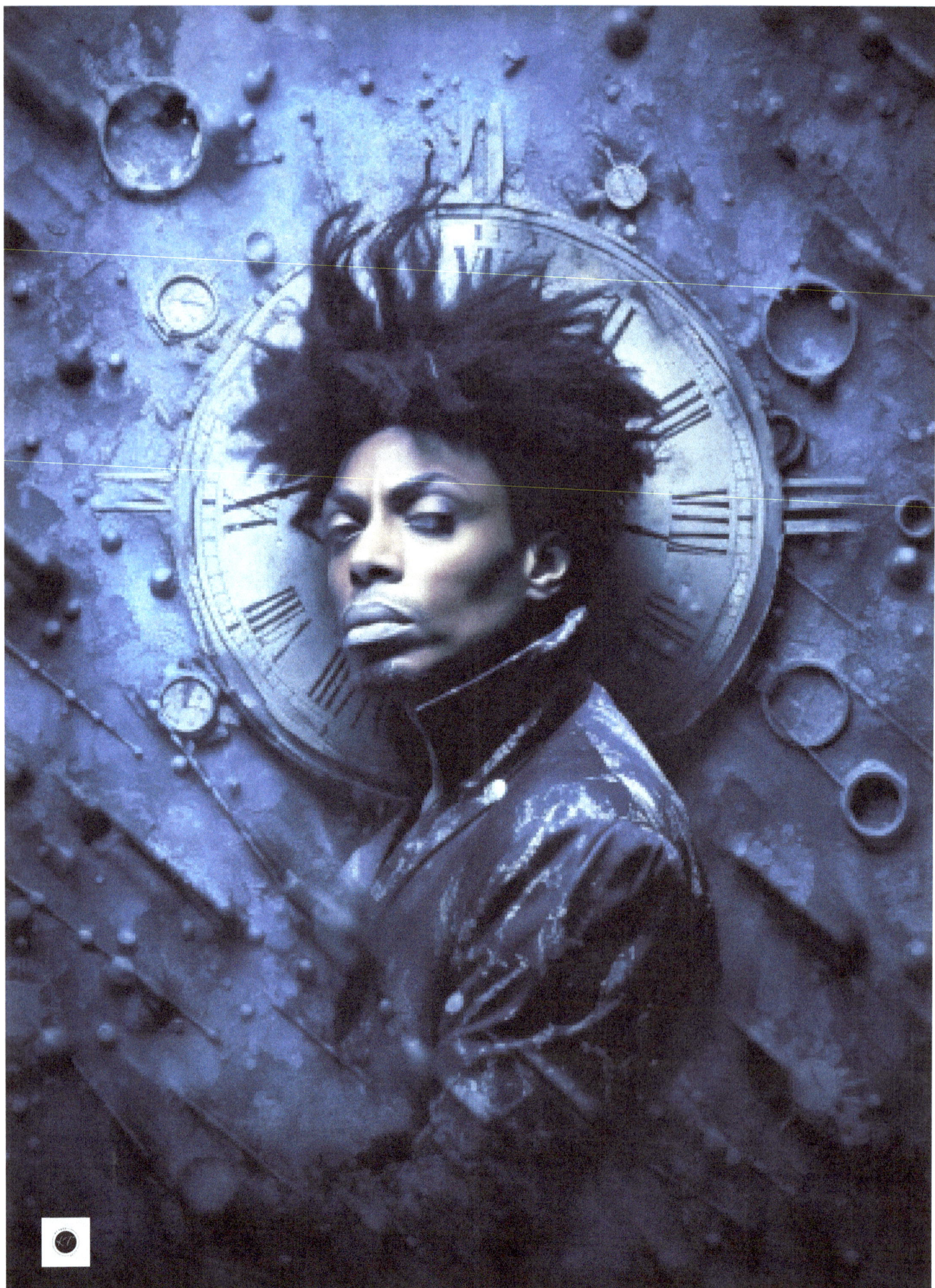

Little Richard

Little Richard as a high-energy sprinter would emphasize his exuberant spirit, groundbreaking performances, and ability to captivate audiences with his flamboyant style and innovative music. Sprinting is a sport that requires a combination of power, speed, and explosiveness, which aligns with Little Richard's talent as a pioneering musician and his iconic status as the architect of rock and roll.

As a sprinter, Little Richard would showcase his determination, focus, and ability to electrify audiences with his dazzling performances, much like how he revolutionized the world of music with his groundbreaking sound and his unwavering commitment to artistic expression. He influenced Elvis, Prince, Michael and Jimi Hendrix. He put the I in ICON.

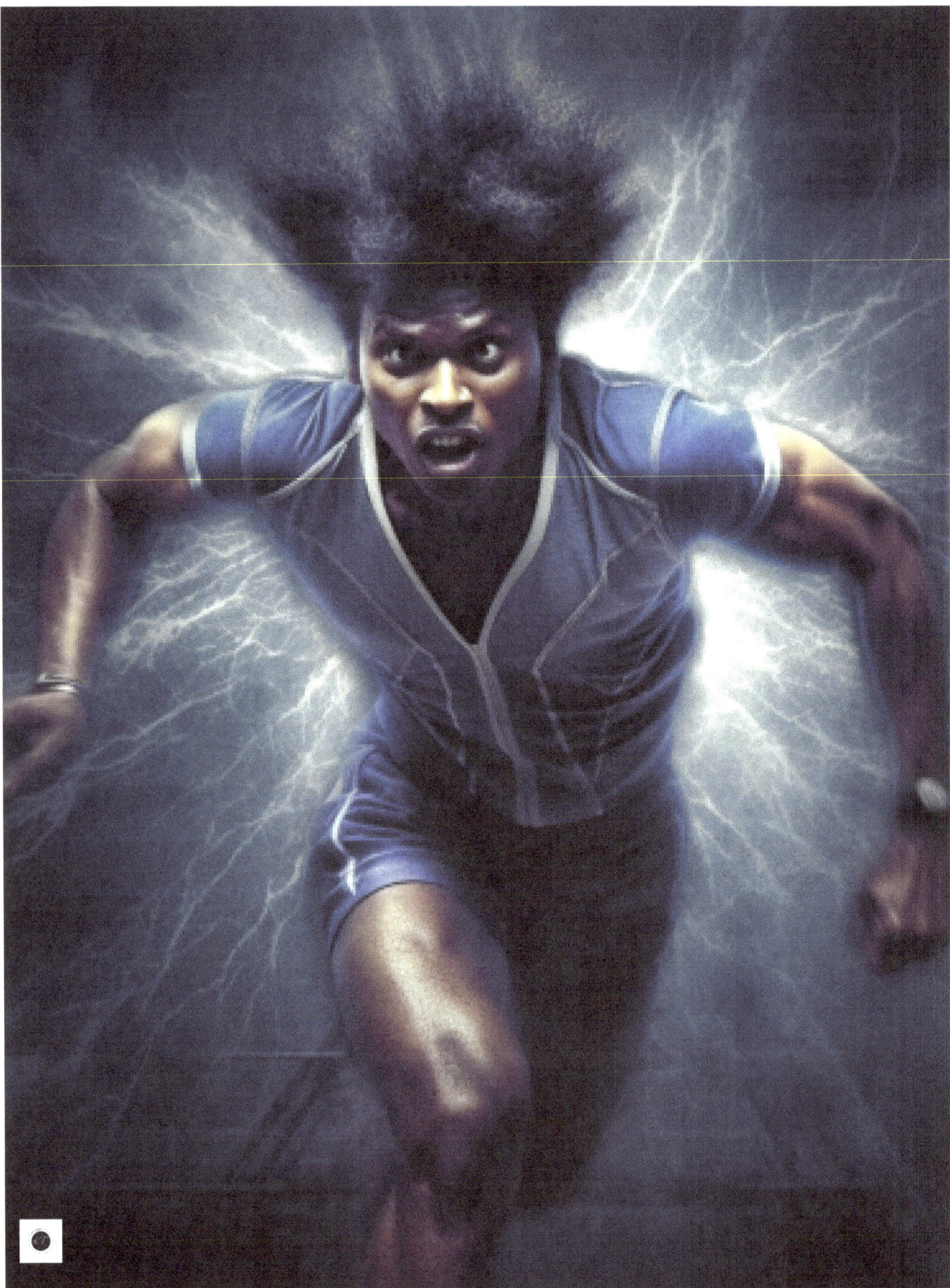

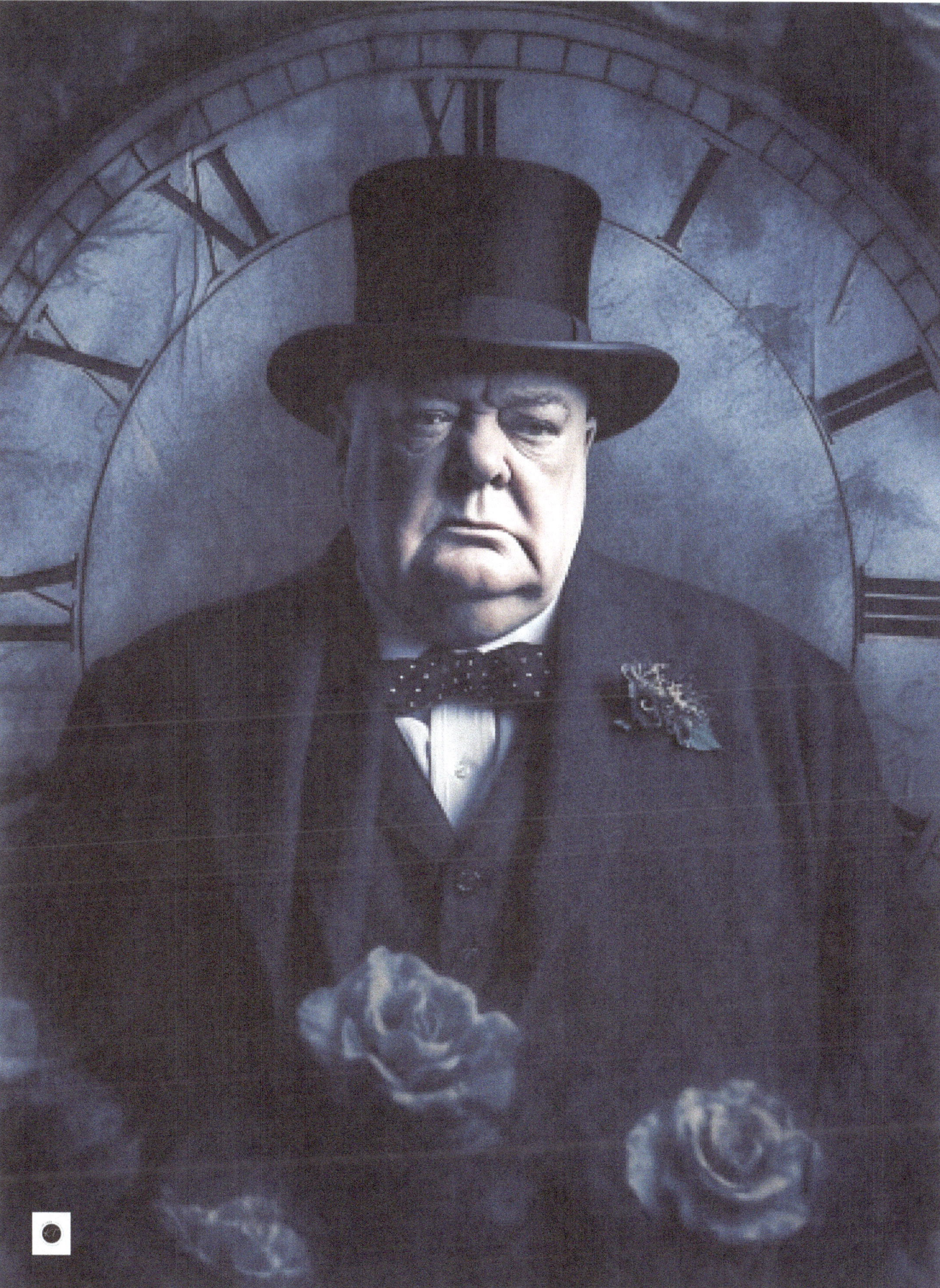

Winston Churchill

Winston Churchill as a strategic board game player (like Risk) would perfectly capture his strategic mind, relentless spirit, and his leadership during the challenging period of World War II. These games require a combination of skill, strategic foresight, and patience, aligning perfectly with Churchill's qualities as a wartime leader and iconic statesman.

As a strategic board game player, Churchill would display his tactical mind, patient determination, and ability to anticipate and counter the moves of his opponents, much like how he navigated the complex political landscape during the war and led his nation to victory. Would that all wars settled over a board game.

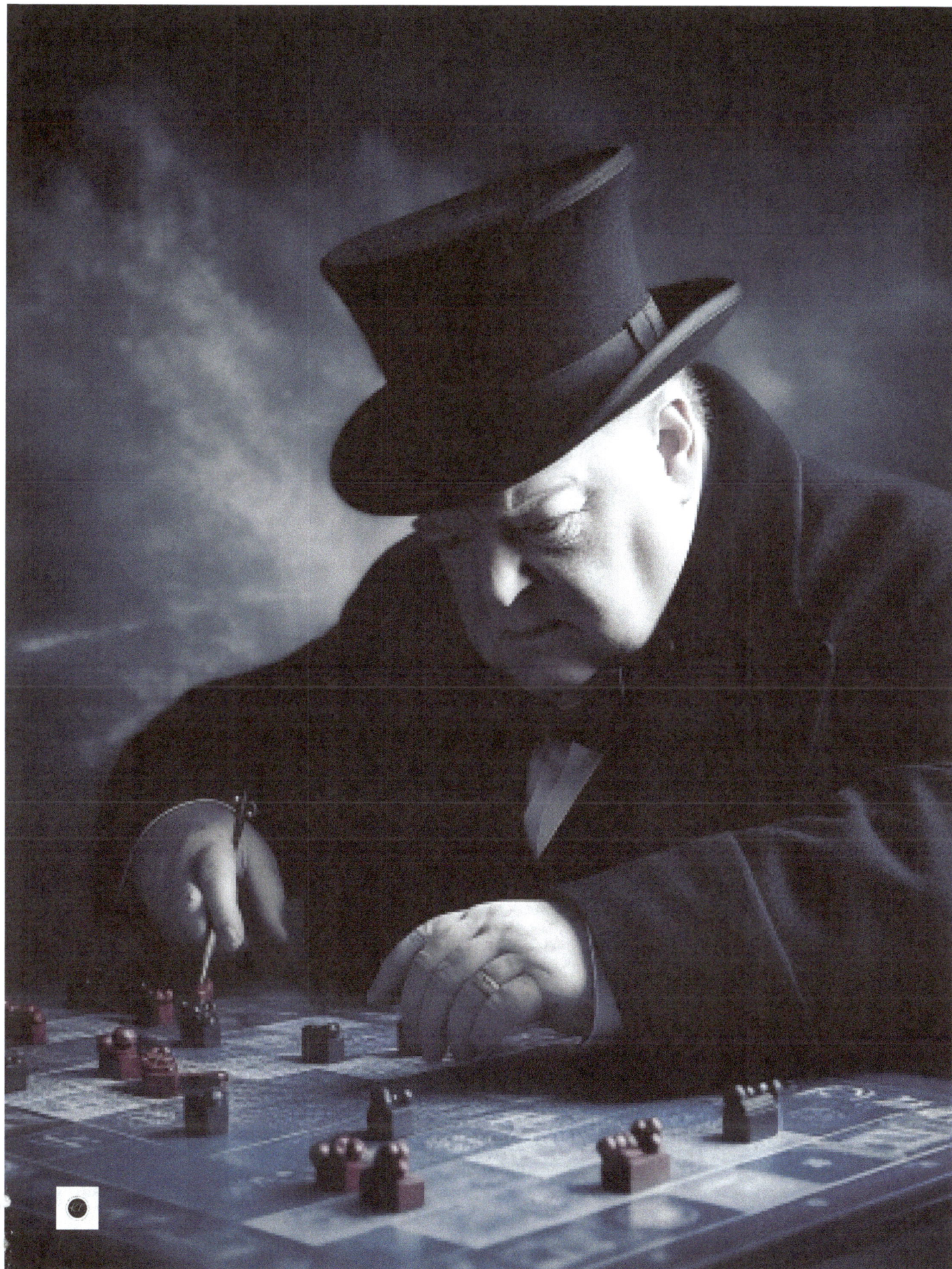

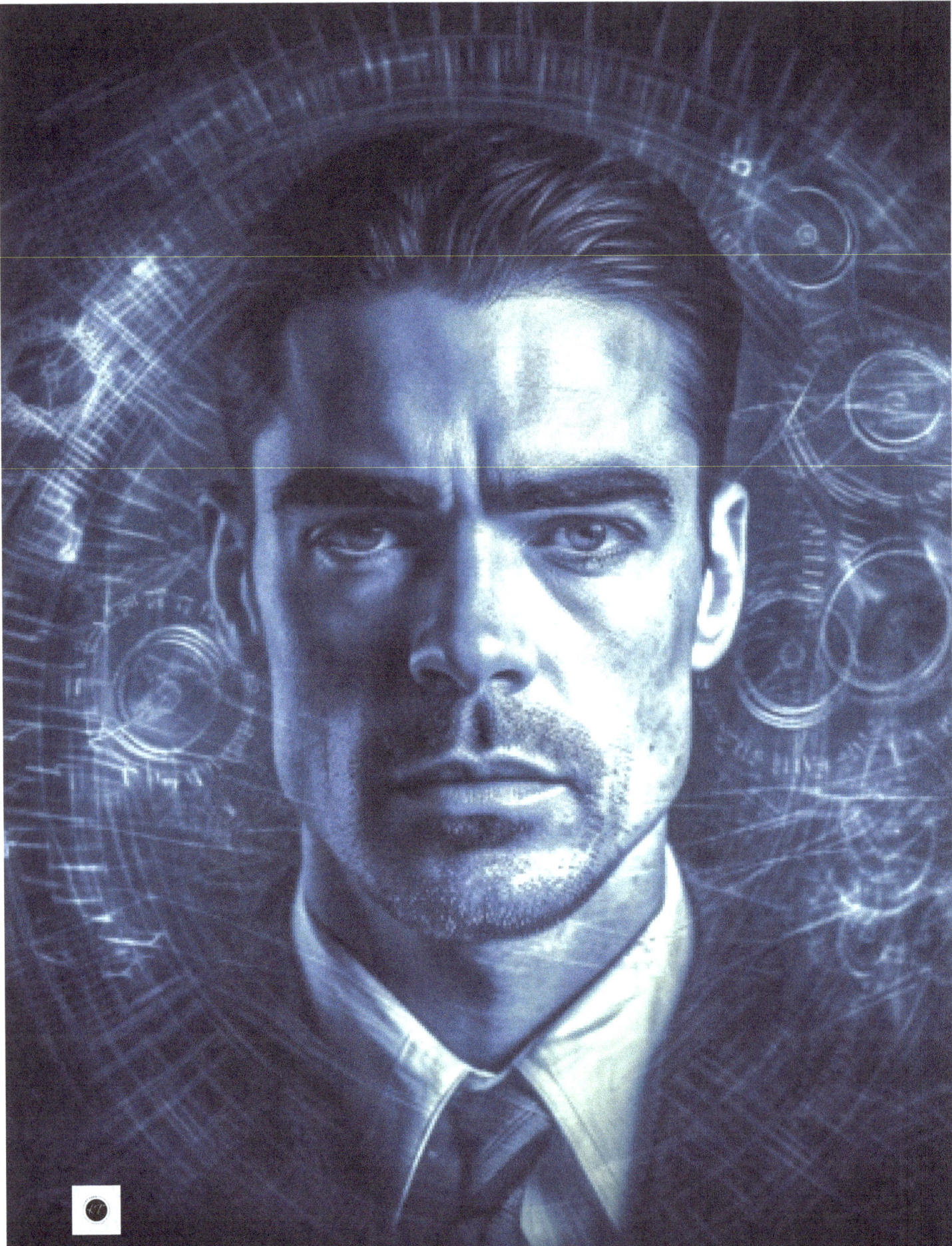

Howard Hughes

Howard Hughes as an air race pilot would perfectly encapsulate his adventurous spirit, innovative mind, and his daring approach to both business and personal pursuits. Air racing is a sport that requires a combination of skill, courage, and strategic thinking, which aligns with Hughes' talent as an aviator,
filmmaker, and entrepreneur.

As an air race pilot, Hughes would display his audacity, focus, and ability to approach challenges from unique angles, much like how he navigated the world of aviation and Hollywood with his innovative ideas and bold investments.

He was Elon Musk without 10 children!

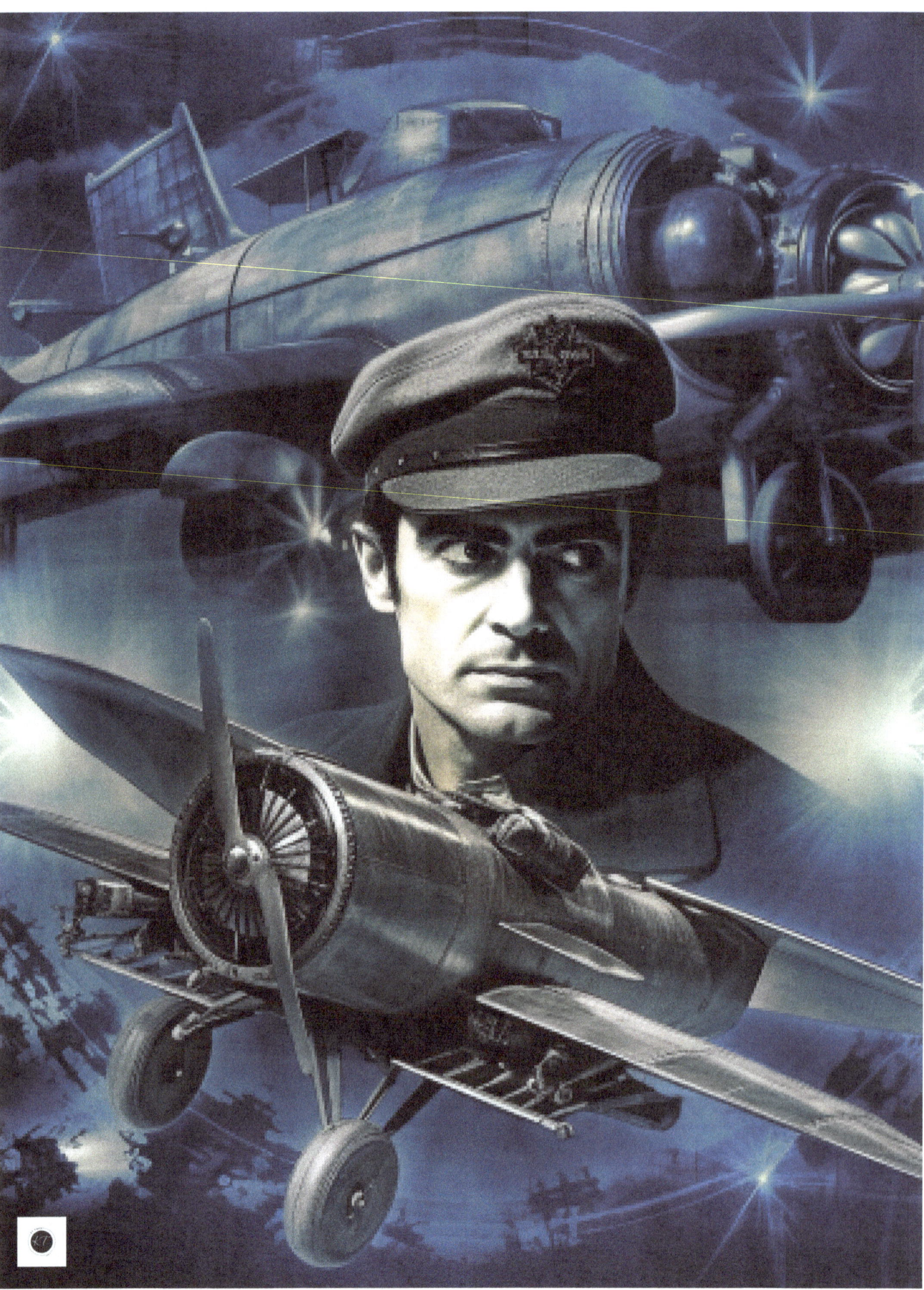

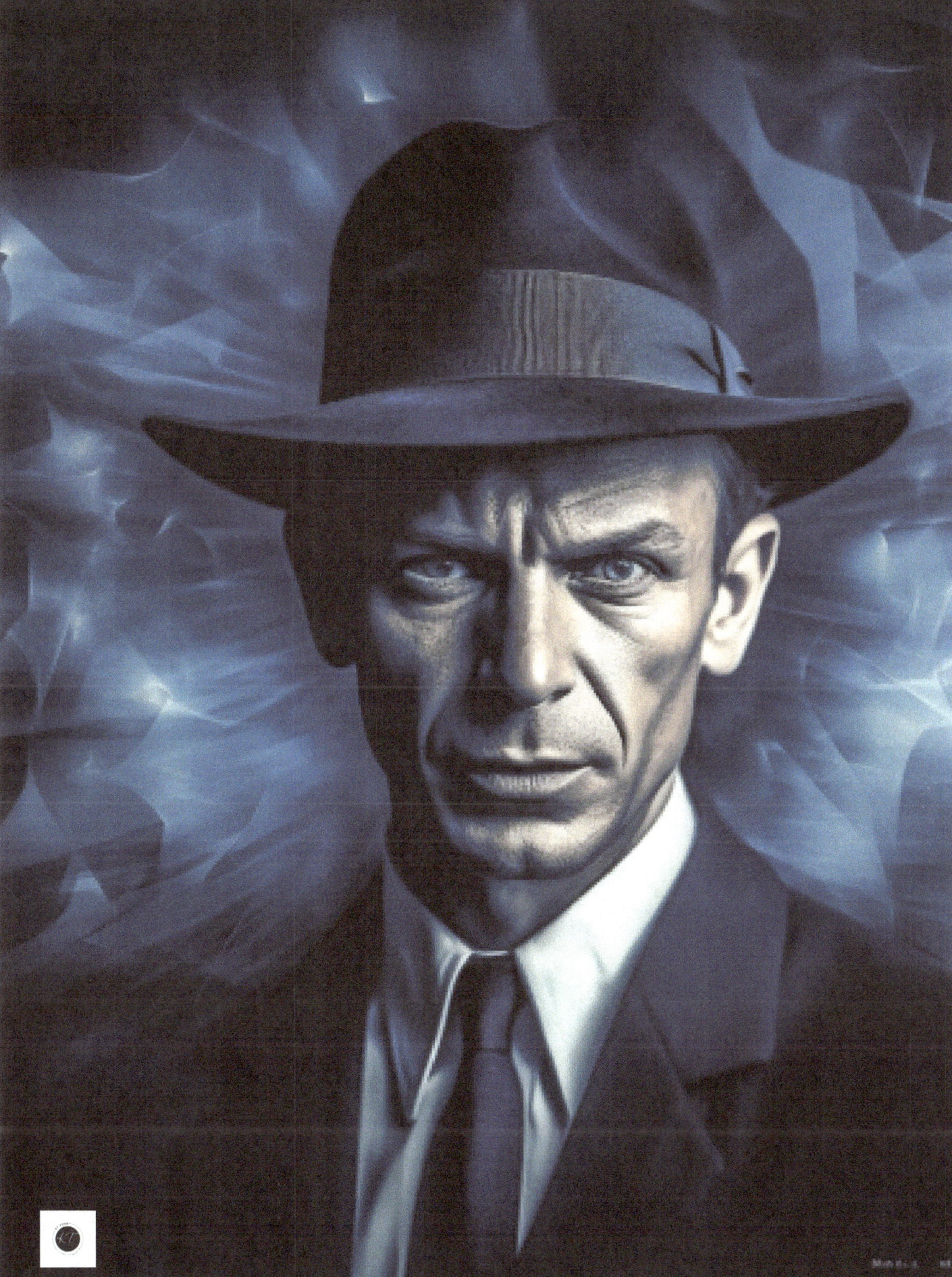

Frank Sinatra

Frank Sinatra as a golfer would be a fitting choice that reflects his personality and life. Golf is a game that requires skill, patience, finesse, and a deep understanding of the game's nuances, much like Sinatra's approach to his music.
As a golfer, Sinatra would display his cool demeanor, precise timing, and strategic approach, much like how he mesmerized audiences with his unique vocal stylings
and charismatic performances.

This role would also highlight his capacity for concentration, his ability to perform under pressure, and his drive for perfection, as golf is a sport that demands a high level of skill, mental strength, and precision. Old Blue Eyes, would be an interesting name for a gangster, just saying.

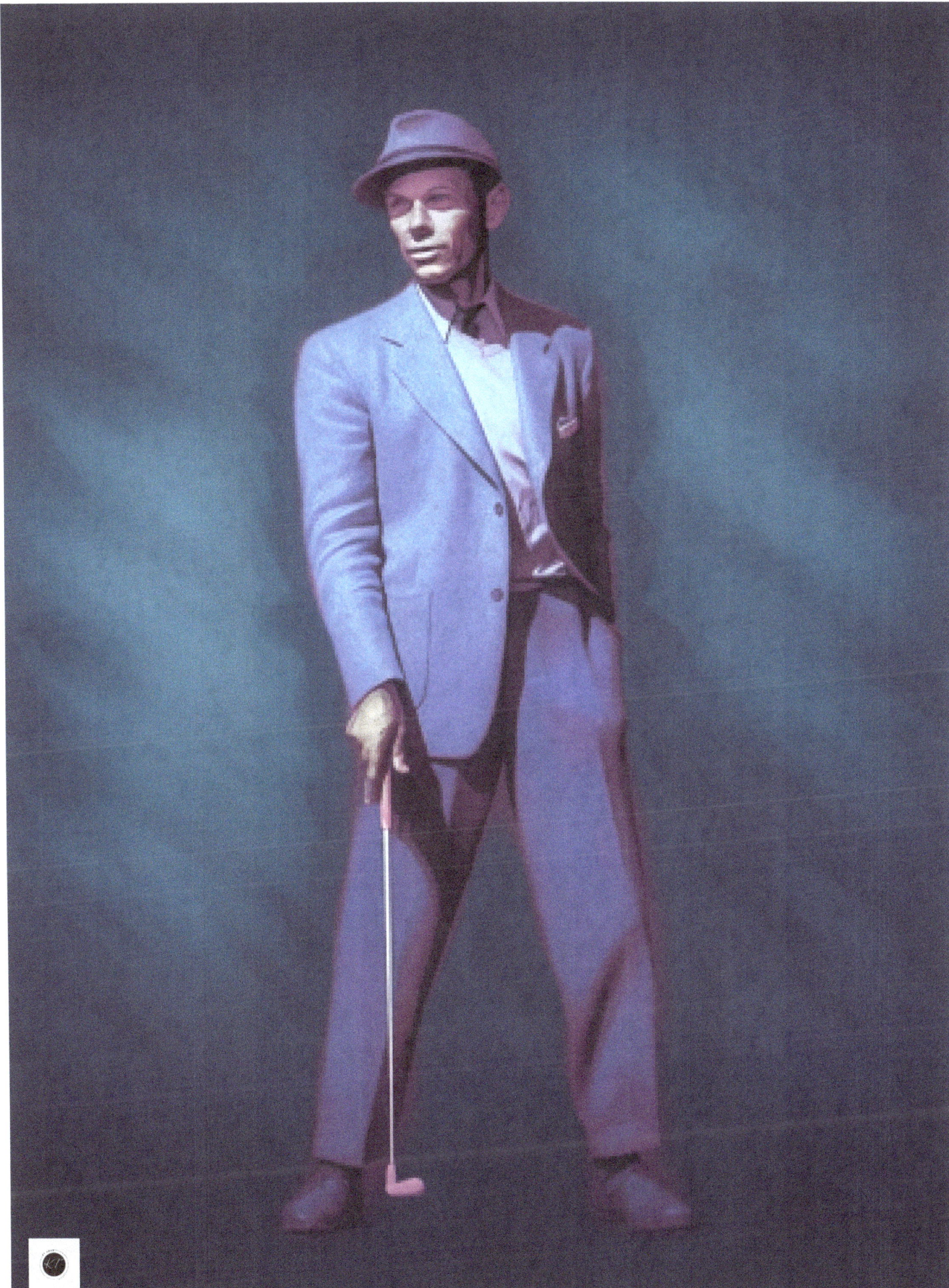

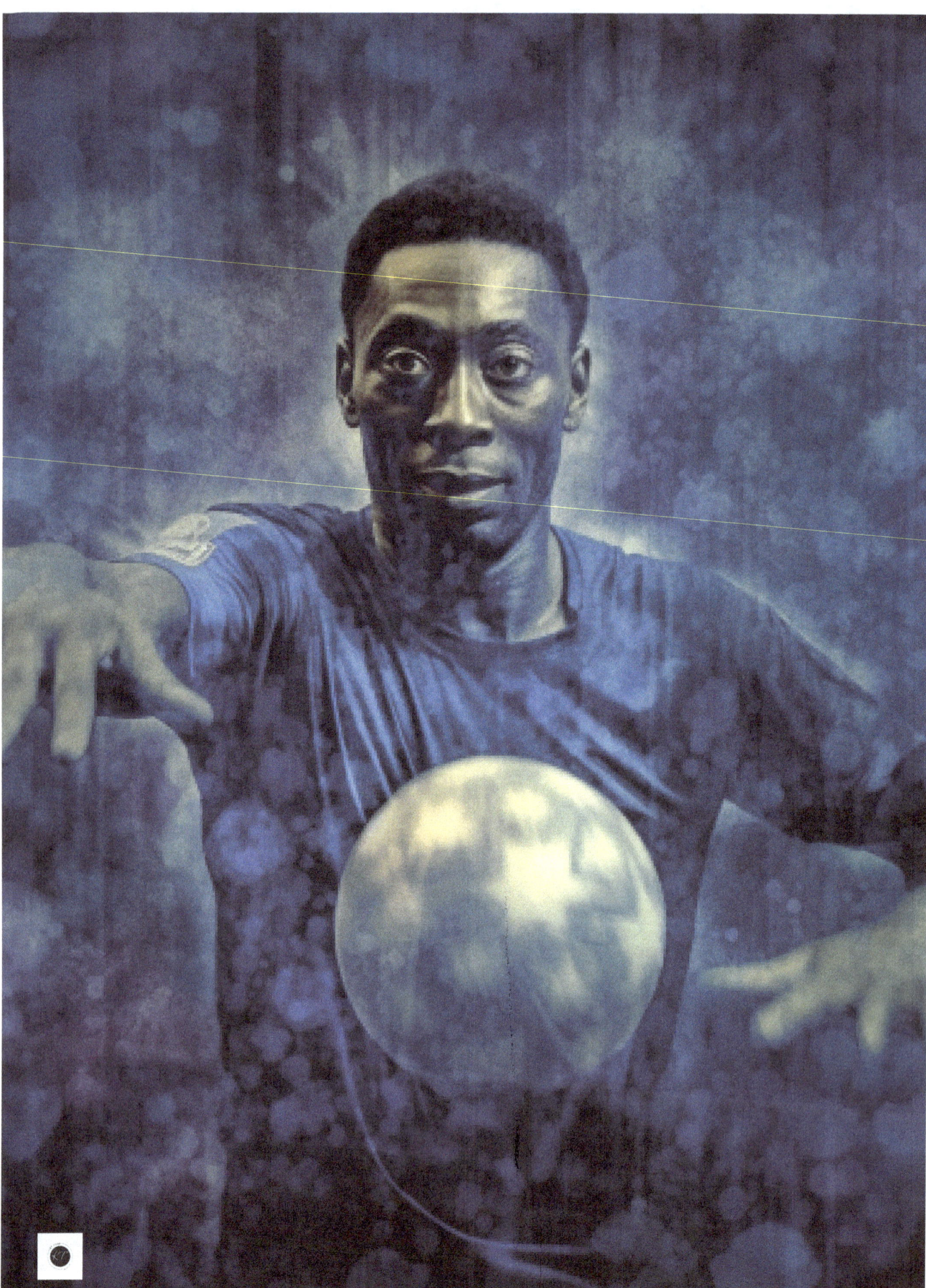

Pele

It would be would be fitting for Pelé to play a percussion instrument that is central to Brazilian music. Bongo's in Brazil is used in various styles of music like samba and capoeira. Playing them requires rhythm, coordination, and a sense of timing – qualities that Pelé displayed on the soccer field. Moreover, the bongo's significance in Brazilian music and its ability to set the rhythm and pace mirrors Pelé's cultural impact and his role as a pace-setter in soccer.

As a bongo player, Pelé would be seen as a maestro, setting the rhythm and the pace, much like how he dictated the flow of the game on the soccer field.

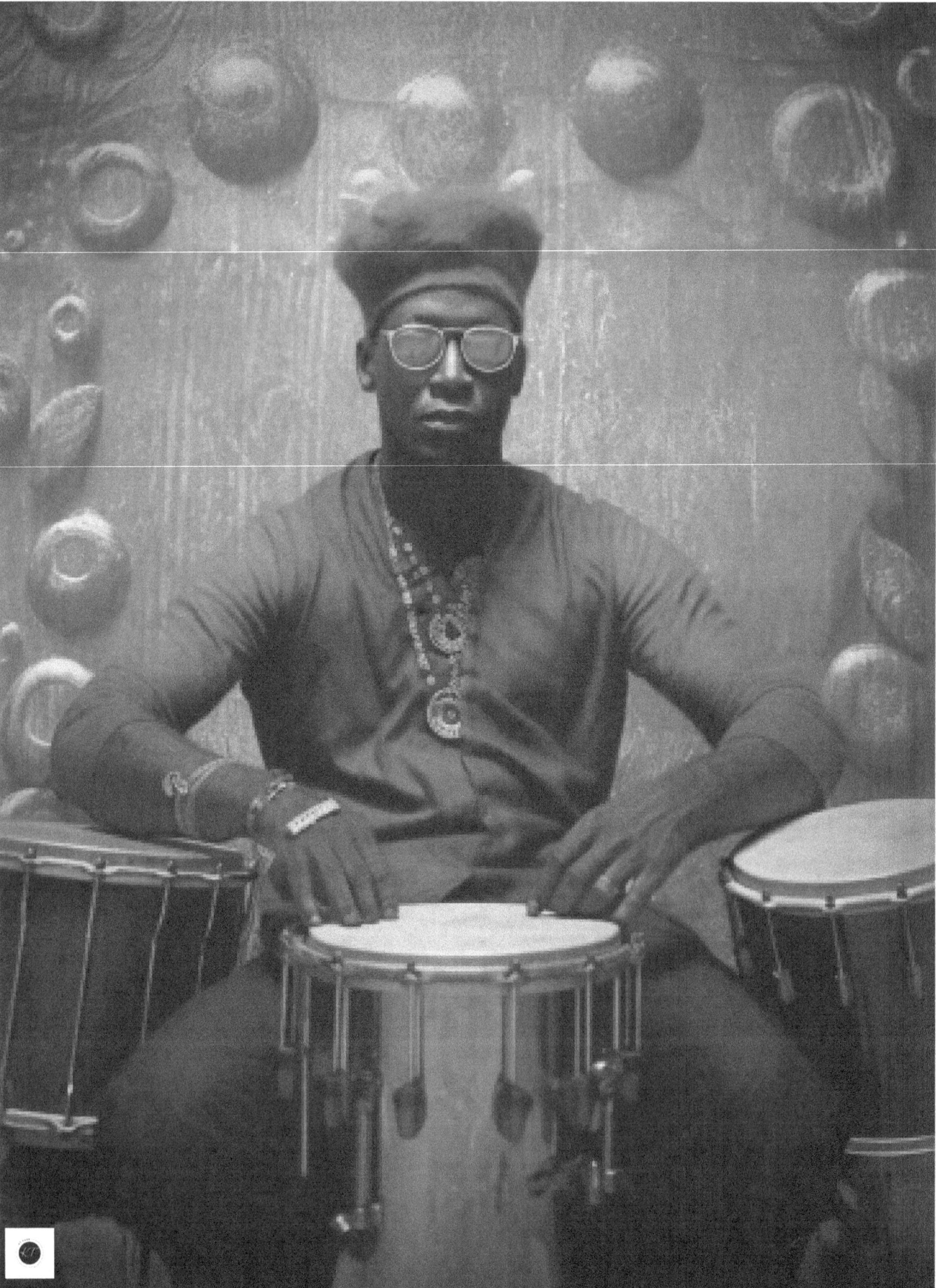

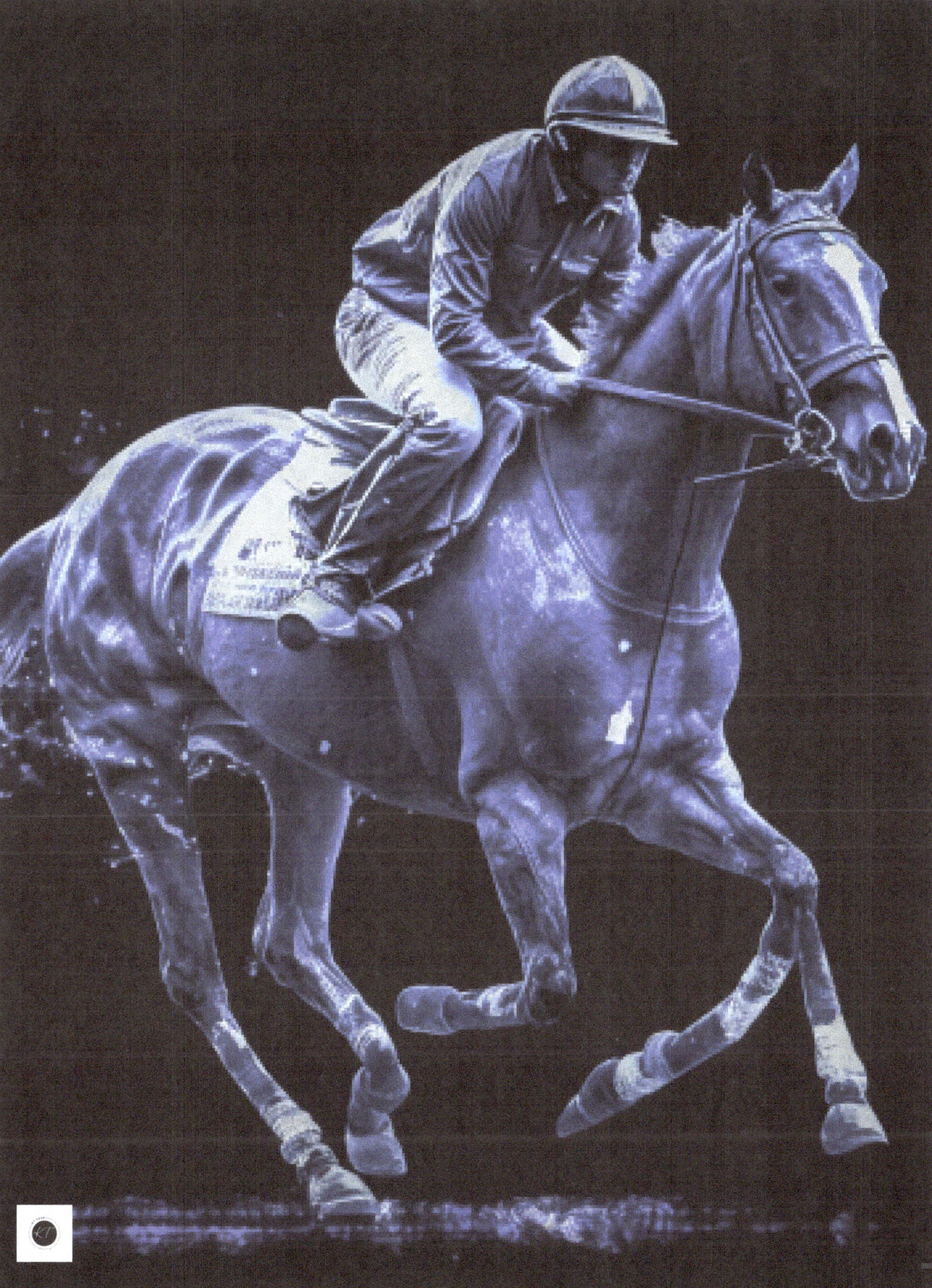

Secretariat

If Secretariat were not a racehorse, he could be imagined as a show-jumping horse. Both disciplines showcase a horse's athleticism, agility, and grace, and they require a strong bond between horse and rider. These qualities align with Secretariat's natural talent and his ability to perform at a high level. He also had an exceptionally large heart, discovered at his death.

As a show-jumping horse, Secretariat would display his power and speed by navigating a course of jumps, demonstrating his agility and precision in clearing the obstacles. This would emphasize his exceptional physical abilities and adaptability. YES, A HORSE, GET OVER IT.

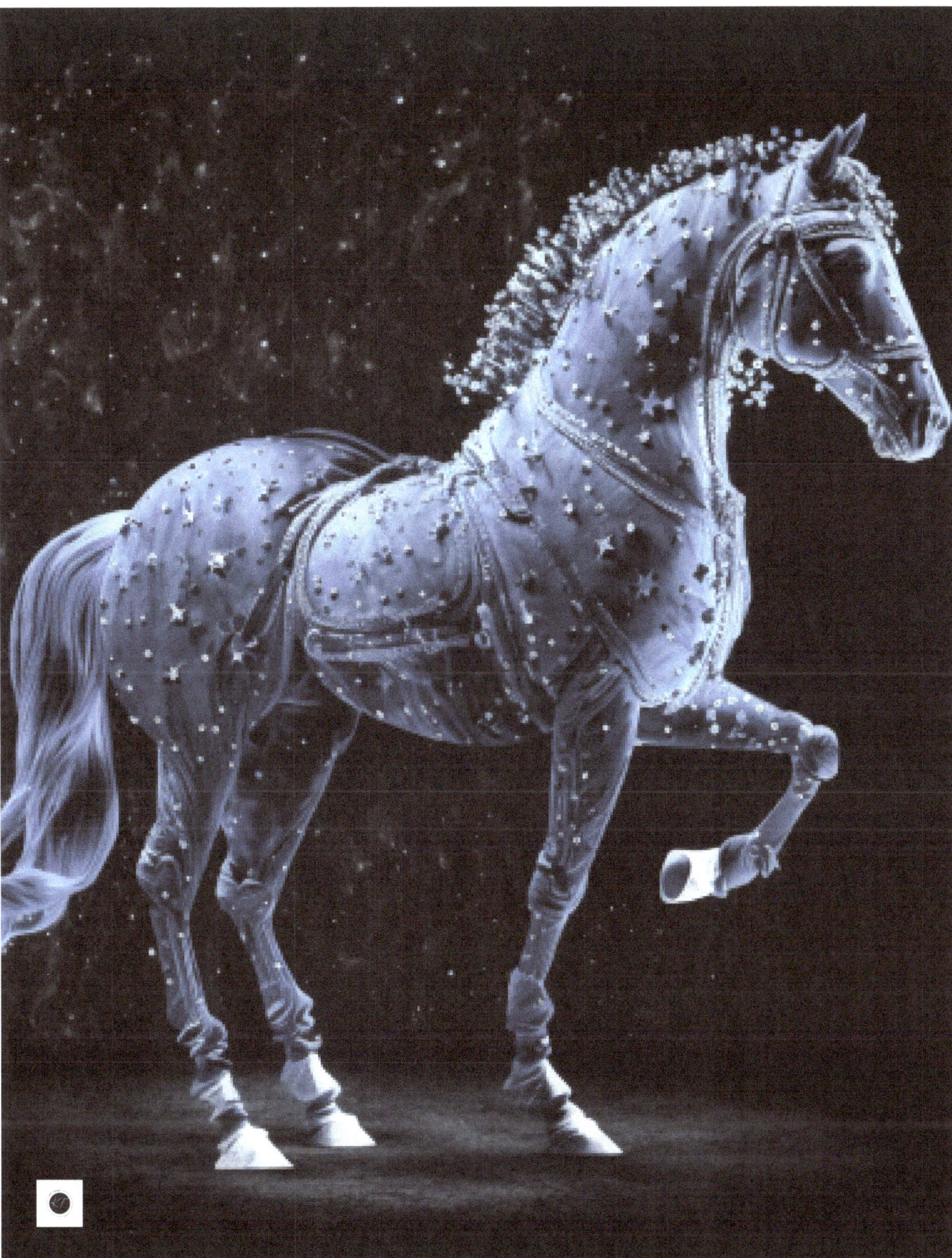

ALL IMAGES CREATED USING THE AI TOOL: MID-JOURNEY-KTF